ANGEL

ANGEL
OF
DEATH

JOHN ASKILL &
MARTYN SHARPE

Michael O'Mara Books Limited

First published in 1993 by
Michael O'Mara Books Limited
9 Lion Yard
Tremadoc Road
London SW4 7NQ

A CIP catalogue record for this book is available from
the British Library

ISBN 1–85479–182–6

Designed and typeset by Florencetype Ltd,
Kewstoke, Avon
Printed and bound in Great Britain

Contents

The authors are grateful for the help they have received from the families touched by the events recorded in this book.

1. The Unthinkable

Peter Phillips struggled to fight back the tears as he carried a tiny Christmas tree, complete with decorations, into the graveyard. Despite his slight frame Peter was fit, active and physically strong which had stood him in good stead when he'd worked as a lorry driver. At forty he still had the impish good looks and sense of fun that had captured the heart of his bride, Sue, when she was just half his age. Now he was broken and so, too, was she.

Sue, blonde, pretty and slightly taller than Peter had been just seventeen when they'd met. He was thirty-four, twice divorced, with two daughters aged eleven and nine at home. Three years after their wedding Sue gave birth to son James and they'd been blissfully happy, though now, on this cold, sunny December day, she battled to keep a brave face as she walked by his side, her mind numb with despair.

When James was three they had been blessed with twins, daughters Becky and Katie, a gift from God. But, as they picked their way through the tombstones, they began to question what kind of a God was this that could give and cruelly take away so quickly.

Quietly, with the watery winter sunshine reflecting on the new white marble headstone, Peter placed the miniature Christmas tree on one side of Becky's grave and laid a small posy of flowers on the other, determined that their baby should not be allowed to miss out on what would have been her first Christmas. Hardly a word was spoken between the two parents as Sue, tears gently rolling down her cheeks, laid a huge wreath, in the shape of a giant teddy bear, on the newly made grave. Becky had only been nine weeks old when Peter had watched her die. She'd been screaming in his arms, her face contorting in agony.

Now Becky lay at peace in this quiet corner of Lincolnshire, in the churchyard behind St John's Church, Manthorpe, on the outskirts of Grantham. She'd been buried in a tiny white coffin, lined with pure white duck down, with two teddies from her cot placed alongside her, and Sue had tossed a red rose into the grave as they'd lowered her coffin into the ground.

The grief had almost been too much to bear on that awful April night when she'd died. But there had hardly been time for Peter and Sue to mourn or ask questions before suddenly, and without warning, twin sister Katie had been struck down too. Katie's life had hung by a thread on that same dreadful day. Sue and Peter had been in torment because, as Becky was lying in the mortuary at one end of the Grantham and Kesteven General Hospital, Katie was fighting to survive on Ward Four, the Children's Ward, at the other end. Fran-

2

tically doctors, nurses and the hospital emergency team had worked on, finally succeeding in saving Katie.

Afterwards, the doctors, who could find no other cause, said that Becky had died from a 'cot death', but they couldn't explain what had happened to Katie. Now it was almost Christmas and, as Sue and Peter arrived at Becky's grave, they were just thankful they still had Katie alive.

Thirty miles to the north, Robert Hardwick pushed his disabled wife, Helen, in her wheelchair towards the grave of their eleven-year-old son Timothy. Helen had been perfectly healthy, full of vitality and energy before she had become pregnant, but then she'd suffered a stroke just two weeks after Timothy had been born. Six months later doctors confirmed that baby Timothy was also terribly handicapped. But, for all that, Timothy had been a joy. Now her son lay buried in the cemetery at Chilwell, on the outskirts of Nottingham, and, as it was Christmas, they wanted to offer a silent prayer for the child they had lost. Timothy, their only son, had died unexpectedly on Ward Four of the Grantham and Kesteven General Hospital.

Little Liam Taylor was seven weeks old when his mum Joanne had taken him to Ward Four. He hadn't been critically ill. The family doctor had been treating him for a bad cold but, when it didn't improve, he diagnosed bronchiolitis, a severe chest infection, and, finally, their health visitor suggested little Liam needed to go to hospital. It was simply a precaution but, within forty-eight hours, he was dead. Doctors diagnosed a massive heart attack though they were unable to discover what had caused it. Liam was buried in the graveyard at St Sebastian's church, in the village of Great Gonerby, just outside Grantham. The white marble head-stone was engraved with a teddy bear and bore the inscription: 'Little Child Come Unto Me'.

In the village of Balderton, fifteen miles north of Grantham, Sue and David Peck were battling to come to terms with their loss. Daughter Claire was their first and only child, a treasure, always laughing, so full of life. She was fifteen months old and just beginning to talk. She had gone into Ward Four in the throes of an asthma attack. The family doctor had told them it would only be a short hospital stay and that she would soon be home. Then, inexplicably, she'd died. The specialist had put his head in his hands and said it was a chance in a million that they had lost her.

In sixty days in February, March and April 1991, three babies and an eleven-year-old boy had died. Nine other children on Ward Four, the youngest aged eight weeks and the oldest six years old, had suffered unexplained cardiac arrests or respiratory failures and recurring fits. There had been twenty-four incidents.

Normally, the hospital's casualty 'crash team' would expect to be summoned to one or two life-threatening emergencies each year on Ward Four, but they had never been so busy, never been called out so often, never saved more children, lost more children, than in those hectic months.

In rapid succession Kayley Desmond, Paul Crampton, Henry Chan, Bradley Gibson, Katie Phillips, Christopher Peasgood, Christopher King, Patrick Elstone and Michael Davidson had become very ill. Some had recovered quickly. Others had been to the brink of death but survived, so near to dying that clergymen had been called to christen them where they lay in the hospital, nurses stepping in as makeshift godparents.

What made it worse for most of the parents was that their children had been in no real danger until they were placed in the care of the hospital.

Doctors were baffled. Could it be some kind of 'bug', affecting children only in one ward of the hospital? Ward Four was swabbed inch by inch and the walls scrubbed. They thought it might be a deadly strain of meningitis or even Legionnaires Disease, but when they found nothing the ward carried on as usual.

Could it be just bad luck? Some of the nurses thought it was simply a run of tragic events. After all, they were treating sick babies and children, and sometimes they died.

No one suspected that the unthinkable could be happening – that there was an evil serial killer stalking the ward, poisoning children and babies.

It took the death of Claire Peck, the fourth victim, finally to convince the hospital authorities that it was time to call in the police. Questions would later be asked as to whether they should have reacted sooner and whether lives could have been saved. But when the hospital made the call to Grantham police station, no one knew what was happening or why.

The Detective Sergeant who came to the hospital listened to the unfolding story in amazement. He went back to the police station and told a colleague: 'I'm out of my bloody depth here.' This was a job for his bosses in headquarters at Lincoln, twenty-five miles away to the north.

Three days later, on 1 May 1991, alerted to the suspicion that something very strange was happening, Detective Superintendent Stuart Clifton, head of Lincolnshire CID, arrived to probe the bizarre sequence of events on Ward Four at the Grantham and Kesteven General Hospital.

More than most Stuart Clifton was a cautious man, a meticulous investigator with a startling eye for detail. He was not immediately convinced that there had been foul play. A lifetime as a policeman had taught him not to jump to conclusions and murder in a children's ward seemed an unlikely possibility here in rural England. Or was it?

If someone was trying to kill babies and children in the hospital, Supt Clifton wanted to know why, as much as how? What kind of person could do such an awful thing? Were they mad, driven by some dreadful demon? Or were they just bad?

Surely it could not be a nurse or a doctor? Nurses worked long hours for little reward and were affectionately called 'angels'. They were rightly held in the highest esteem. But, if it was not a nurse or a doctor, then who else had access to the ward? Supt Clifton was accustomed to investigating robberies and murders where there was always a motive. It could be greed, it could be love or jealousy, that had been the spur, but what could cause someone to kill and keep on killing one helpless infant after another, attacking others, week after week, for sixty days? Later, much much later, psychiatrists were to come up with a theory.

Not much happens in Grantham and locals are almost proud of the fact. The ancient, red-brick town which stands beside the notoriously dangerous A1 London-to-Edinburgh trunk road, the Great North Road, has a population of 30,000 and a reputation for being the dullest place in Britain. More than 1000 of its residents thought it was so boring they wrote to the BBC in a nationwide poll in 1981 to claim the title. Some even suggested the best thing to come out of Grantham was the A1 itself.

But it's a prosperous market town, big enough to command its own Marks and Spencer store, a large Boots the Chemists and Woolworths, and a spacious indoor shopping centre with a multi-storey car park, all set on either side of its one main shopping street.

On Saturdays, market-stall holders take over

Westgate and Market Square. The town still boasts two Grammar schools, the King's School for Boys, founded in the sixteenth century and the Kesteven and Grantham Girls' School, plus several other secondary schools and a modern College of Further Education.

The surrounding peaceful, rolling Lincolnshire sheep country, winding lanes and unspoilt villages, was the childhood playground of Margaret Thatcher, Britain's first woman Prime Minister. Her father, Alfred Roberts, a town Alderman and Mayor of Grantham, paid £900 for a corner shop in North Parade, not far from the town centre, in 1919 and ran it as a greengrocers, tobacconists and sub-post office.

Her father sold the shop in 1959 as a going concern for £3500. Nowadays the old shop is a high-class restaurant, aptly named The Premier, and many of the original fittings remembered by schoolgirl Margaret Roberts have been restored and preserved. Across the road is a new development of homes, called Premier Court. The town likes to remember its handful of famous residents.

During the plague year of 1665 Sir Isaac Newton watched an apple fall from a tree at his home just outside Grantham, and established the law of gravity. Modern-day jokers, fuelling the story of the town's boring image, unfairly say the falling apple was probably the most exciting event ever to happen in the town. Now there's a statue of the legendary mathematician on the green outside the Guildhall, there is a new shopping mall named in his honour, the Isaac Newton Centre, and also the Sir Isaac Newton pub where you can drink to his memory. His family home, Woolsthorpe Manor, is owned by the National Trust and open to the public.

Modern, bustling Grantham, the administrative centre of the south-western corner of Lincolnshire, known as South Kesteven, has a high-speed rail link to London's Kings Cross station, taking just an hour, and maintains its links with the surrounding farming communities with a Cattle Market on Thursdays. In the town centre stands the Angel and Royal Hotel, one of the oldest coaching inns in Britain, dating back to the twelfth century, a wonderfully preserved relic of the days when Grantham was important as a staging post for travellers on the Great North Road. The inn, which still has a set of medieval stocks by its main entrance, proudly boasts several Royal visitors in the past, including Richard III, King John, Charles I and Edward VII. On the opposite side of the High Street stands the George Hotel which was mentioned by Charles Dickens in his novel, *Nicholas Nickleby*.

About a mile out of town, on the road north to Lincoln, is the Grantham and Kesteven General Hospital, its stone and red-brick facade set behind pretty, well-kept flowerbeds. Like many small-town hospitals, the friendly, 120-year-old complex has spread over the decades and now consists of a maze of added-on buildings, including some new structures built since 1981. Now builders were back again, constructing a huge new extension at a cost of £5.5 million on the town side of the complex behind a notice board which announced proudly: 'New Hospital for Grantham. Opening May 1992'.

By the entrance to the original Victorian building are Wards Nine and Ten, occupied mainly by geriatric patients; a long, wide, cream-painted corridor leads straight ahead, brown direction signs hanging from its ceiling. There's a spur off it to the pathology laboratory on the right and doorways on the left to the cardiology unit, orthopaedic ward and Wards One, Two and Three.

Halfway down the corridor a smaller corridor leads to the old out-patients department and, further on, another spur goes to the hospital chapel, the midwifery school and the entrance to the modern, three-storey maternity unit which attracts mums-to-be from a wide area around and as far away as Newark in neighbouring Nottinghamshire.

At the very far end of the long corridor, where the colour of the paint changes from cream to light green, opposite an old, original red telephone box, well used by parents and relatives, is Ward Four, the Children's Ward, a cosy, friendly place with large windows, where colourful paintings and pictures drawn by children adorn the light-green walls.

It is divided into two smaller wards, one with six beds and the other with four, with three consultancy rooms, a kitchen, a large playroom full of toys, games and a TV to occupy the young patients and visiting children, a treatment room with specialist equipment for emergencies and six individual rooms, called cubicles, for children who were more seriously ill.

It was here, early in 1991, while the world's eyes were fixed firmly on the War in the Gulf, that youngsters began collapsing in numbers never seen before.

Sue and Peter Phillips first met on 26 June 1985 at the Grantham and Kesteven General Hospital, a remarkable coincidence for the hospital was to play such a huge part in the tapestry of their marriage.

At seventeen, Sue was attractive with blue eyes. She had just broken off an engagement. Lorry driver Peter, at twice her age, was divorced from his policewoman wife and was playing the role of mother and father to his two daughters, Nicola, eleven, and nine-year-old Emma.

Sue had gone to the hospital to visit friend Simon Howlett in Ward Two and remembers instantly feeling sorry for the 'poor bloke' in the next bed whose face was in a terrible mess. Peter had been attacked and beaten up – left with a broken nose, broken ribs and cuts and bruises all over his body.

She offered to walk with him down to the rest room so he could smoke a cigarette. Romance followed quickly. Three months later she moved in with him, quickly taking over the role of homemaker and mother to his daughters. They were happy and comparatively well off. Peter was working as a farm driver and she carried on her job as a computer programmer at Edisons, a fork-lift truck-hire firm in Grantham.

They were married on 7 June 1986 at the town's rather smart registry office, less than a year after their first meeting. They lived in a rented cottage in the village of Sedgebrook, on the Duke of Rutland's estate, and were allowed to use the Duke's ancestral home, fairytale Belvoir Castle, as the romantic backdrop for their wedding pictures. It was a blissful start in some of England's most beautiful countryside, famous for its fox hunting. Often in the village they saw Prince Charles, riding with the Belvoir Hunt and, occasionally, a glimpse of Princess Diana on a visit to the castle.

They both wanted a baby but, as is often the case with eager couples, it didn't happen easily. They had to wait nearly two years. The birth of their first son, James, on 8 April 1988 took Sue back to the Grantham and Kesteven Hospital.

Sue had become seriously ill while she was pregnant and doctors at the hospital couldn't decide why. She was sent to St Thomas's Hospital, London, where specialists identified the germ causing the problem. It wasn't a minute too soon. The couple were told that Sue's life had been in jeopardy and there was a real danger she would lose the unborn baby. If she became pregnant again, her life could be at risk. Sue was allowed back to Grantham where, despite the fears, James was born safely by emergency caesarian in the maternity ward on the first floor.

When, two years later, she became pregnant again, Sue remembered her experience with James's birth and decided to have the pregnancy terminated. It just wasn't worth the risk and her family doctor agreed to send her to the termination clinic. Sue recalled: 'It was awful. I sat there with a load of thirteen- and fourteen-year-old girls, crying their eyes out because they'd got into trouble.

'I didn't like what I was doing but I knew I would be risking my life to go on any further.

'When I got to see the doctor he insisted on giving me a scan. It was just part of the process as far as I was concerned, ready for the termination.'

Sue, now twenty-two, was not expecting the shock news the doctor gave her. First, he told her, she was thirteen weeks pregnant, not just two months as she expected. She knew the baby was now fully formed and instantly she felt it was too late for an abortion.

Secondly, the doctor announced, it was *twins*.

Sue said: 'I was just numb. I had spoken to Peter before about abortions. We both said that we would never consent to a termination once the baby was fully formed because it would be like murder. We couldn't do that. But then it was twins too.

'I went straight to see him at work and I told him he had better sit down. I said, "I'm thirteen weeks," and he said "Oh! my God." He knew what that meant. Then I said: "There's something else. I'm expecting twins."

'He just sat there, his mouth was just open and he said nothing. It was ages before he spoke. Then he said: "Oh my God," again. But we both knew what was going to happen, that we would go ahead with having them and we just started to plan for two babies.'

They decided to invest in a new home, a modern, five-bedroomed house in a cul-de-sac just half a mile from the gates of the hospital. It was the roomy house they needed with a fast-growing family. There was a bedroom for themselves, one each for Nicola and Emma, another for baby James and the fifth . . . the new nursery for two.

Peter decorated the 'twins' room', chosing neutral colours because they didn't know whether to expect boys, girls or one of each. They splashed out on a twin pram, twin buggy, two cots, matching baby seats, two sets of baby clothes, double the number of bottles. They had got over the initial shock and were getting excited about the prospect of twin babies in the house.

Sue had to go into hospital in January 1991 for a rest and observation after doctors discovered sky-high blood pressure; although the babies were not due until April she was transferred to the specialist baby unit at Nottingham City Hospital where doctors prepared to deliver them early by caesarian section.

On 31 January the twins were born. They were both small, Becky weighing 3lbs 2ozs and Katie was even smaller at 2lbs 12 ozs. Both babies were put into incubators and were ventilated because of their premature arrival; they were fed through tubes. But they were healthy and doctors told Peter and Sue there were no fears for their safety.

How wrong they were to be.

At that time the couple were busy running a car-valeting company in Grantham, cleaning and polishing second-hand cars ready for the show-rooms. It was Sue's brainchild to start the business on an industrial estate in Grantham, and it became so successful that Peter gave up his driving job to join in. With Becky and Katie still in hospital building up their strength, Sue went back to work.

But a chance remark by a customer signalled the beginning of the nightmare that was eventually to devastate their lives. He told her: 'Hey, Sue. Your babies are in the hospital, aren't they? Well, a pal of mine's baby has just died there. The baby had some sort of massive heart attack.'

2. Liam – 'Little Pudding Pants'

Baby Liam James Taylor was affectionately called 'Pudding Pants' by his parents because he was so chubby. He was just seven weeks old, a lovely, healthy boy, born in the maternity ward at the hospital weighing 9lbs 3ozs. He was Chris and Joanne's second child, a little brother for Jamie who was three years old.

He put on weight in the early weeks but then developed a worrying, heavy cold and, when it showed no sign of improving, Chris and Joanne called their family doctor. He made made several visits to their semi-detached home in Grantham, and diagnosed bronchiolitis. Despite the medications that were prescribed Liam still showed no sign of improving, and when the family's health visitor popped in the following week she advised Joanne to take him to the hospital where he could be properly monitored.

It wasn't an emergency and it wasn't even a major crisis when Liam arrived at hospital and was admitted to Ward Four, the children's ward. He was poorly, but not in any kind of danger, and everyone thought he would be home in a couple of days. Being in hospital was 'only a precaution', not life or death. Joanne, slim, with short blonde hair, was reassured. After all, wasn't Liam safer in the children's ward than anywhere else?

She and Chris could never have known the anguish that was soon to follow.

Tall, dark-haired Chris was busy at work as a suspended ceiling fitter when Liam went into hospital. He arrived home soon after 3pm on 21 February to find a note from Joanne pinned to the front door saying she had taken their little boy to Ward Four at the hospital. Chris didn't wait to change from his work clothes and went straight to the ward. He needn't have rushed. By the time he got there Liam seemed to be getting better already.

He was lying in a glass-sided incubator, dressed only in his nappy, and was smiling happily, seemingly over the worst of his problems. The staff had placed him on a nebuliser which fed him oxygen to clear his nasal passages and chest. One nurse reassured Joanne: 'Don't worry, he'll be home in four or five days.'

A young, heavily built nurse with cropped blonde hair was looking after him, supervising his feed through a tube because Liam was so congested he couldn't suck from a bottle. Nurse Beverley Allitt had been given the job of caring for Liam on a one-to-one basis.

She was a newly qualified State Enrolled Nurse who had been been turned down just five days earlier for a job in the children's ward at the Pilgrim

Hospital in Boston, thirty miles away. They'd told her she didn't have enough experience treating very sick youngsters.

All her life Beverley Allitt had longed to be a nurse; it had been her consuming passion, her only ambition, since she was a child, but more than anything else she had set her heart on nursing children. She had always had a special affinity with youngsters, everyone knew that.

The young nurse, still only twenty-two, had trained for three years at Grantham and spent the last six months as a student with the children on Ward Four; as the ward was short of staff, she was asked to stay on. The hospital had advertised for a Staff Nurse but hadn't received a single application and so she'd been given a contract for six months. It would be six months in which she could learn. Then she could re-apply for the job at Boston six months later.

Beverley Allitt had taken the opportunity to gain the experience she needed and was determined not to waste a single day. On Ward Four she found herself in charge of caring for the newly admitted infant Liam, feeding him through a tube as his parents watched.

All was going so well that Chris, still dressed in his work clothes, was happy enough to leave the hospital with Joanne to go home and change. They were gone an hour but, when they returned, they were greeted by a nurse with unexpected bad news. She told them: 'We have been trying to ring you. We are glad you've come back because Liam has taken a serious turn for the worse.'

Chris and Joanne went to the cubicle where Liam was being treated. Something had happened in the short time they had been away and Liam was suddenly fighting for his life. He had changed beyond recognition. His eyes were closed, his face grey and it looked as though his whole body had just 'shut down'. He was covered in wires to his chest, attached to heart monitors and a drip into his arm.

Joanne burst into tears and had to be comforted by a nurse. Nurse Allitt was standing in the door-way to Liam's room with her arms folded in front of her.

Joanne asked her what had happened while they were away and the nurse told her: 'While I was feeding him he was violently sick. It was so bad I had to go and change my uniform.'

The couple listened with growing unease as Allitt told them that their baby had actually stopped breathing for a minute because he was being so sick. They took an instant liking to the young nurse who was being so open with them. In the difficult hours that lay ahead they felt she would be an ally and friend.

The hospital had two paediatric specialists: Dr Nelson Porter and Dr Charith Nanayakkara, a Tamil known to most at the hospital as 'Doctor Nana'. They were both experienced doctors, used to handling emergencies, trusted by parents. Neither of them could have foreseen the appalling events that were now beginning to unfold on their ward.

It was Dr Nanayakkara who arrived that afternoon to tell Chris and Joanne that the next twenty-four hours would be crucial for baby Liam. Nurse Allitt continued to care for her tiny patient on a one-to-one basis until 10pm when she went off duty.

The Taylors were no strangers to the hospital. Chris's father had worked there as head porter for sixteen years and Joanne's mother was a ward orderly. Through the night, with another nurse now monitoring his progress, Liam was getting better. His vital signs were looking more healthy and Chris and Joanne were able to snatch some sleep in a room down the corridor reserved for parents.

The next morning Nurse Allitt came back on duty at 7am and took her place again at the bedside. Liam was on drips and there were tubes feeding him. By now, Chris and Joanne had come to rely on the girl who had become 'Liam's nurse'. They didn't like the thought of Liam being without her and, when one nurse went sick, Chris asked Allitt to return and work an extra night shift to care for Liam. Chris asked her: 'Would you please come back and look after him?'

Nurse Allitt went off duty at around midday, promising to return for the extra night shift. While she was away, Liam got progressively better. At 3pm he actually smiled; then, at one point, he stretched out as if he was trying to reach for his teddy.

He was so much better that he was moved into Mr Happy's Room — a cubicle with the smiling figure of the 'Mistermen' character painted on the window. Joanne said later: 'I felt pleased that he had been moved. I remember thinking: "Oo! Look. They're putting him in Mr Happy's Room." It seemed a good sign.'

The staff kept praising Liam. He took some feed out of a bottle, opened his eyes wide until they looked as big as saucers, kicked his legs to try to shake the monitor wires free, and cooed at the nurses and his parents. It was as if Liam wanted to tell the world that the worst was over.

Relieved at his improvement Joanne decided to go home and tell the neighbours and their friends waiting for news that Liam was getting better. As she drove home from the hospital Joanne suddenly found herself crying tears of joy.

Nurse Allitt returned to the ward at 10pm ready to stay at Liam's side throughout the night. By this time Joanne had returned to the hospital. Content in the knowledge that he was in safe hands and pleased at Liam's recovery, she went down the corridor at 10.30pm to try to catch up on some sleep in the parents' room.

Husband Chris remained at Liam's side and chatted with the nurse, asking if she had managed to sleep. But she said she had gone shopping instead. Eventually, at around 1am he, too, went to bed, confident that Liam was going to be all right.

That night the world was plunged into war in the Gulf – Saddam Hussein snubbed the 'High Noon' deadline and the battles began. But the peace of Chris's and Joanne's sleep was shattered at 5.30am when they were woken by Sister Jean Saville, the hospital's night services manager and the most senior nurse on duty. She told them that the news was bad. Liam had suffered a relapse.

She said: 'I am sorry, your baby has just stopped breathing for a few minutes and the doctor is with him.'

Chris and Joanne rushed down the corridor to Mr Happy's Room. The room was packed with people, all crowded round Liam's incubator. Dr Nanayakkara was already there, along with Nurse Allitt and the hospital emergency team. Liam, they were told, had suffered respiratory failure but was now breathing again. He was alive, but only just. He was lying on a resuscitaire, being given oxygen, with drips attached to his body feeding him drugs.

Quietly, the specialist told them the dreadful news that he believed Liam had suffered severe brain damage, caused by a lack of oxygen when he had stopped breathing. Now he was critically ill. Chris and Joanne were devastated by the sudden and unexpected catastrophe. When they had gone to bed Liam was getting better, and now here was the doctor saying his life was in the balance. Even if Liam lived the damage to his brain meant he would never be the same again.

Chris and Joanne were asked if they wanted the chaplain, the Rev. Ian Shelton, to christen Liam. When they agreed he arrived minutes later from his home opposite the hospital. Only Joanne, Chris and the chaplain were in Mr Happy's Room as he

22

conducted the short christening service in which the baby was named Liam James Taylor.

The couple went to see Dr Nanayakkara in his office. Chris asked: 'How severe is the brain damage?' The doctor told them that, in his professional opinion, it was severe. He said that Liam had stopped breathing for a considerable period of time.

'Normally, in children who have respiratory failure, their condition can be stablised in a matter of minutes but, in Liam's case, it took 1 hour 15 minutes.'

The parents' world was suddenly in pieces.

Chris later said: 'I turned to the doctor and asked: "Are you telling me we have to decide what we are going to do?" He nodded "Yes." '

Now they had to face an awful dilemma. Was it best for Liam to die, rather than endure a lifetime of suffering? They discussed their options, deciding that all that mattered was doing their best for Liam. 'We went off to the canteen on our own and we decided then that he had been through enough.'

Joanne remembers turning to Chris and saying: 'This is meant to be. Our little boy has tried to leave us once, and the doctors have pulled him through, but now God is taking him back . . . I felt then we should let nature take its course. I remember thinking, why does God want him back? Why can't he take our house, anything, but not our baby?'

Quietly, they agreed that he should be taken off the equipment. They turned to chaplain Ian

Shelton and asked him if he thought they were making the right decision. 'He told us, in the circumstances, he thought we were right, but he couldn't put himself in our position,' said Chris. They told the staff of their decision. Liam's drips and monitors were removed. It was 6.30am.

Chris picked Liam up in his arms and the couple sat together, waiting for the end to come. They were told it would not be long.

But Liam didn't die. Instead, little 'Pudding Pants' was so strong he fought on, clinging to life. They sat cradling Liam in their arms for more than five hours. As they watched and waited they were told that, even without support, Liam was now holding his own.

Then, at about midday, Dr Nanayakkara called them to his office and told them that he hadn't expected Liam to survive so long. He asked them what would happen if he woke up and needed feeding. Chris told him: 'I'll feed him if he has the will to survive. We will help him all we can if he wants to fight.' He later said: 'I couldn't stand to see him suffering for the rest of his life but, if Liam was going to pull through, then we were going to give him every support.'

Consumed by anguish, Chris and Joanne decided to carry on and let nature decide the issue. They asked everyone to leave the room so they could be alone with their baby. About twenty-five friends and relatives had gathered at the hospital, knowing that Liam's life was hanging by a thread, and the pressure on the couple was mounting.

They sat together with their baby son. The monitor, which would have detected the slightest shift in Liam's condition, was no longer there. The nebuliser, which would have fed him oxygen to help his breathing, had been removed. So had the drip which had helped stabilise his condition.

The physiotherapist, who had worked so hard to try to clear the congestion from Liam's chest, wasn't at his bedside any more. Chris and Joanne felt the medical world could do no more for the baby they loved so much. Liam was linked only to a simple alarm which ticked and flashed green each time he took another breath. If he stopped breathing his parents knew the green light would turn red.

Chris and Joanne took it in turns to cradle Liam in their arms, treasuring the precious moment, knowing now that time was running out. Their baby was exactly eight weeks old to the day and they knew, beyond all doubt, that he was going to die.

As the end approached chaplain Ian Shelton arrived in the room to say a prayer for Liam which began 'Little Child Come Unto Me . . .'. Somehow the words were a comfort.

A nurse, who had been so excited the day before at seeing Liam kicking his legs, cooing and smiling from his cot, went off duty telling Joanne: 'I'll see you tomorrow.' But Joanne already knew she would not be there the following day.

'I remember thinking we wouldn't be there when she returned to the ward. I knew Liam wouldn't wake up. It was instinct. His little legs were shaking all the time. His arms were moving up and down. When Chris passed him to me, he was like a rag doll. I was frightened of dropping him. He looked so beautiful, not poorly at all. His nose wasn't blocked any more and his skin was perfect.'

At 2pm the flashing green light began to slow and the ticking began to fade. Chris turned to Joanne and said: 'I think he's going. We told Liam we loved him.'

They had been waiting seven and a half hours, holding their baby in turns. Suddenly Liam took three final deep breaths and the red light flashed on. Only after he had died, when they were absolutely sure he had gone, did they call in the hospital staff who confirmed that Liam was dead. A nurse gently placed baby Liam in a Moses basket, put his hands together and wrapped his little fingers around a tiny posy of small white flowers.

Bewildered by all that had happened Chris and Joanne drove home to the house where Liam's bottle still lay waiting for his next feed.

With Liam gone his parents wanted the answer to only one question. What had caused their little boy to stop breathing so suddenly and without warning, recover briefly and then die in the space of a few short hours? In her torment Joanne was prepared to consider the most bizarre theories. 'I even wondered if it was something to do with me warming Liam's milk in the microwave oven. I'd been scratched by a rabbit during the pregnancy, and I even thought about that and wondered.'

The hospital asked the heartbroken parents for their permission to perform a post mortem to establish the cause of Liam's death and, anxious to help find a reason, Chris agreed. The death certificate, issued by Dr Nanayakkara, had specified pneumonia and suspected septicaemia, but the post mortem, which was carried out under the supervision of the coroner, came to a different conclusion. The pathologist, Dr Terry Marshall, decided Liam had suffered an 'infarction' of the heart; effectively, the muscles of the heart had died.

The coroner's officer, Maurice Stonebridge-Foster, relayed the verdict to Chris and Joanne. He had done his duty and there was now no reason why Liam's funeral couldn't take place. Still desperate for an explanation Chris made an appointment to meet Dr Marshall.

Over a cup of tea in the hospital canteen the pathologist told Chris he did not know what had caused Liam's heart to die. 'He told me it was the sort of thing you would expect to happen to a middle-aged or old person who'd been a drinker and smoker all his life. He simply couldn't explain it happening to an eight-week-old baby boy.'

Chris spent an hour talking to the pathologist but went home with all his questions still unanswered. A night or two later he watched a TV documentary about heart attacks. Afterwards, Chris phoned the programme makers to ask: 'Have you ever heard of a little baby being killed by a heart attack?' They, too, were at a loss to explain why Liam had died. After all, they said, it was virtually unknown for the muscles of a baby's heart to die. It was terribly sad, but they couldn't help any more.

Dr Nanayakkara was so disturbed that he wrote to the coroner saying that he was unhappy with the finding of the post mortem. He told Chris that he was sure that it must be something else. He wanted a child pathologist called in to perform a second post mortem. 'He was frustrated and annoyed because they wouldn't let him study the findings on which the original result had been based.'

Chris and Joanne were resigned to the fact that they might never know what had really happened to their baby on Ward Four.

Liam was cremated on Friday, 1 March at Grantham. It seemed right that Ian Shelton, the chaplain who'd whispered words of comfort when Liam was close to death, should conduct the short service.

Liam's ashes were buried the next day at the parish church in Great Gonerby on the hill above the town. A white, marble headstone, carved with a sleeping teddy bear, marks his tiny grave. The epitaph, carved in the headstone, reads:

Liam James Taylor
Pudding Pants
Died 23rd February, 1991

Aged seven weeks
Love you hundreds
Mummy, Daddy and Jamie
Little Child Come Unto Me

If events on Ward Four had ended there, the real cause of Liam's death would probably have remained undetected. Nothing had come to light that could explain why he had suffered such a massive heart attack.

3. Timothy – 'My Special Boy'

Then, on 5 March, just three days after Liam had been buried, another child died on Ward Four.

Timothy Hardwick, the second victim, was eleven years old but he was just as helpless as baby Liam. He'd been born with severe brain damage and had never been able to talk, see or walk. In many ways he, too, was still a baby like Liam, incapable of questioning his treatment.

His life had been tragic from the beginning. Mother Helen and father Robert, thirty-six, longed for a son. Helen already had a healthy six-year-old daughter, Elaine, when she found out that she was pregnant again; a scan revealed it was a boy, the child that would make their family complete.

The Hardwicks were thrilled and Helen, at thirty-four, was full of energy and vitality, eager for the birth. The pregnancy was uneventful in the early stages but, with only a fortnight to go, Helen fell seriously ill and had to undergo delicate surgery to remove fluid from her brain. The operation was a success and there was no panic, no drama, when Timothy was delivered by caesarian section at the Peel Street Hospital for Women in Nottingham on 25 January 1980. He was a bonny little boy, perfect in every way, or so it seemed.

The operation and subsequent birth had taken their toll on Helen and it was decided she would need time to regain her strength before going home to care for Timothy. She was transferred to a convalescence hospital at Bulwell on the outskirts of Nottingham but, as Helen began to recover, excited at the prospect of being at home with her baby, she suddenly, and without warning, suffered a stroke.

When she came round the left side of her body was paralysed. Helen didn't know what had happened; only that she had lost all the feeling in her face, left arm and leg. Gently, the doctors broke the news that she would never be the same again. The stroke had left her crippled and epileptic. Helen would have to spend the rest of her life confined to a wheelchair, only able to walk a few steps unaided. In the end Robert would be forced to take redundancy from his job as a railway guard to look after his wife.

Timothy was not to escape the tragedy of his birth. He had been a beautiful baby, outwardly perfect, with a smile that would melt hearts in the years to come. But, as the weeks turned into months, it became obvious there was something wrong and the doctors said they would have to carry out tests.

The news, when it came, was devastating. Helen was told that her little boy had been born severely handicapped. He was epileptic. Worse still, the doctors found Timothy was suffering from cerebral palsy and blindness.

Helen had every right to feel bitter; lesser women would have crumbled in the face of such an appalling tragedy. But no, she said, Timothy was a gift from God, important and wonderful to her.

From the outset it was clear that Helen could not bring up the baby she loved. She wanted to care for Timothy from her wheelchair, but it was just too much. So, at five weeks, Helen and Robert placed their son in the care of the county council. At first he went to live with foster parents, but even they could not cope. Timothy was moved to Cordwell House, a children's home at Southwell, twenty miles from Nottingham. Despite his enormous problems he flourished and Helen and Robert were proud as they watched him grow.

Helen, slightly built with long, dark hair, smiled as she recalled his love of music and passion for disco dancing in his wheelchair. He had been so good at it he'd won first prize in a competition for disabled children. He couldn't see or speak, but Timothy at least could hear. And his face would light up at the sound of music.

'Some people might expect me to feel bitter. After all, before he was born, I was just a normal, healthy woman. As a girl I'd passed my ballet exams with honours, then I'd worked full time in my father's shop, I'd always been full of life, but the stroke left me an epileptic and handicapped.

'But I don't blame Timothy for any of this. I'd always wanted a son and when they did the scan, and said I was expecting a little boy, I was absolutely thrilled.'

Helen would never know what had caused the stroke. 'The doctors could never say for certain. It could have been the birth that had brought it on, or the operation I'd had a couple of weeks before Timothy was born. Nobody has ever been able to say.'

Timothy would never talk, or be able to put one foot in front of the other and walk. The doctors told Helen and Robert he was blind. 'They told us he could not see, but we always wondered because he used to blink when a camera flashed. He had all those problems, yet he was a beautiful little boy. He was a gift from God and a joy to us, despite everything.'

As the years passed Helen and Robert remained close to Timothy, never missing his birthday or Christmas, travelling to the home to join in the fun. Often he would be brought to their home for day trips. Elaine loved her younger brother. They were the best times for Helen and Robert.

'Timothy gave so much of himself to everyone. I felt honoured to be his mum. He loved swimming. They had a pool at the home and he really liked splashing about with the other children. He loved horseriding, too. It was hard for him to sit up straight when he was on the horse's back, sometimes he would fall forward and bump his nose on the saddle. He used to love the smell of the horses and, when they trotted, he used to laugh out loud.'

Timothy's problems didn't extend to his appetite.

He loved Weetabix, beans and hot chocolate. Each day staff would take him to the Applegate School in Newark. He loved the journey, bouncing up and down in the minibus. At school he made friends.

Though he was now eleven Timothy could do little for himself. He still couldn't feed himself or go alone to the toilet. But the staff at the school, and at the home, were rewarded. Helen explained: 'He couldn't do anything for himself, but Timothy had this way of giving love to others. One of the staff at the home used to take him to church every Sunday. He loved the organ music and the singing. I'll always remember her saying that, of all the children she had known, Timothy was the one she felt she could adopt.'

Timothy had a habit of smiling at the sound of his mother's voice. 'He couldn't talk, couldn't walk, he was brain damaged and they said he couldn't see either. He suffered from cerebral palsy and he was always in and out of hospital. He had a lot to bear but, for all that, he was a lovely little boy. He used to smile a lot. He always recognised my voice and would grin when he heard it.'

Staff at the children's home recorded Timothy's progress in a scrapbook. They filled it with photographs of him splashing in the pool, riding the ponies and playing with the other children at the home.

Alongside the pictures were poems Helen had written about her boy. Timothy was five years old when Helen sat quietly and penned one such poem, titled, simply, 'Our Special Son'.

Oh Timothy my special boy
How I'd love to see you more,
To see you laugh, and walk and talk perhaps,
Is that too much for a mum to ask?
My Heart cries out for you, my lad,
And so does the heart of your poor dad.

A year later Helen wrote 'My Timothy's Song'.

I wonder what would be my little Timmy's
     song
If only he could speak?
Would it be a happy one,
And one that gladdens everyone?
Perhaps, it would just sadden one to think he
     cannot see,
But to hear my little boy come up to me and
     say,
'Don't worry mum,
'I'm happy, 'cos I know I'm loved by every-
     one.
'Even tho' I cannot see
'Jesus is with me every day
'And night-time when I sleep.'

On Sunday, 3 March 1991, Timothy was brought
home by minibus to spend a day with his parents
and sister. The family enjoyed a walk in the park
and Timothy was his usual self. It was to be the last
time Robert and Helen would see their son alive.

Two days later, on the afternoon of 5 March,
Timothy suffered an epileptic fit while at school

and was taken to hospital in Newark. There was no night shift on duty there so Timothy was transferred to Grantham and Kesteven General Hospital. Nurse Beverley Allitt, the young, newly qualified SEN who had tended baby Liam Taylor, was in the third week of her six-month contract. Liam had been dead just ten days. Now, the same nurse would care for Timothy.

He was doing well and seemed to be getting over his epileptic fit. He hadn't had one for several hours and doctors were pleased with his progress. It was drug-round time on Ward Four, the busy period for nurses, when all the children are given their various medications. Suddenly his condition deteriorated.

By 6.30pm Timothy was dead.

The cause of his death was given as 'epilepsy and cerebral palsy', and some who didn't know him or his parents might have thought it was a blessed release. The day after he died Robert and Helen went to the Chapel of Rest at the hospital to see their little boy. Helen said: 'I could have picked him up and brought him home; he was lying there like a little doll as though he was asleep. I wanted to say: "Wake up! Timothy." '

The funeral service was held at the United Reform Church in Beeston, Nottingham, where the couple were regular worshippers, and Timothy was buried in the graveyard at Chilwell, a few miles away.

As they laid him to rest Helen heard a blackbird singing so sweetly in a nearby tree that it made her turn to Robert and say: 'That's Timothy singing.'

She couldn't help thinking, in a strange but some-how comforting way, that her little boy, who couldn't talk but so loved the sound of music, had found his voice at last.

To his parents, who were both strengthened by their Christian beliefs, there was to be some com-fort. They discovered that both of Timothy's corneas, unaffected by his blindness, had been used in transplant operations. The couple had only too readily agreed to donate them and, some time later, they received a letter from the London Eye Hospital thanking them for the gift which had saved the sight of two total strangers.

Kayley Desmond was fourteen months old and a celebrity in the hospital. She had a cleft palate and couldn't feed properly so, instead of going home, she had stayed in hospital for the first four and a half months of her life before going home.

All the nurses and doctors had known blonde, blue-eyed Kayley almost since the day she was born and her parents Finbar, who was forty-five, and Margaret, thirty-eight, had virtually lived for months beside her bed, first in the intensive care unit and later in Ward Four.

On 3 March, two days before Timothy Hard-wick's death, she was back in hospital, this time suffering from nothing more than a heavy cold, a rattly chest and a cough. Antibiotics hadn't moved the infection, so her doctor decided she would be better off in hospital; Kayley was admitted again to Ward Four.

It didn't take long to get her back on the road to recovery and, after six days, doctors announced that she would soon be home. They were happy with her progress. The day couldn't come soon enough for her parents; Margaret had stayed on at the hospital, sleeping in a side ward and leaving daughter, Zara, aged five to be cared for by babysitters. Husband Finbar didn't leave most nights until 9pm or 10pm.

Then, on 9 March, Kayley collapsed with respiratory failure which struck her, without warning, in the middle of the night. She had two attacks in three hours. Her mother witnessed the first at 1am when she saw Kayley lifting herself in her cot and then keeling over. She'd stopped breathing.

Margaret later recalled: 'I thought she was dead. I thought I'd lost her.' Doctors and nurses dashed to Kayley's side and the emergency team managed to start her breathing again.

Margaret was in the red telephone box in the corridor at the entrance to the ward, telephoning relatives to tell them of the crisis, when Kayley was struck down again with another attack at 4am. This time it seemed that her heart had stopped beating.

Margaret rushed back and police were sent to the couple's home at 5.35am to alert Finbar who, without a telephone at home, had been unaware of Kayley's fight for life. Again, the nurses and doctors brought Kayley round but she was clearly desperately ill. Her brain had been starved of oxygen, which would become an obvious cause for concern later.

Kayley was transferred to the Intensive Care Unit at the Queen's Medical Centre in Nottingham, twenty miles away. There her recovery was swift. By the time Finbar got to Nottingham, Kayley was breathing quite normally with the help of oxygen. He said: 'The police had told me she'd taken a turn for the worse and my heart sank to the bottom.

'I went there fearing the worst and yet when I got there her eyes were open. Within two days she had picked up completely.'

She was taken back to Grantham after three days and eventually allowed home. Later she went into Nottingham City Hospital where surgeons success-fully carried out an operation to repair her cleft palate. But there seemed no explanation for the mysterious two attacks that had nearly ended her life.

Yik Hung Chan was called Henry by his parents. His father Eddie was boss of Mr Pang's Chinese restaurant in nearby Stamford, just down the A1. Henry was two years old, a happy child with a boisterous sense of fun, when on Maundy Thursday, 28 March, he plunged twenty feet out of his sister's bedroom window to the patio below. He was rushed by his frantic parents in their car to the casualty department at the hospital just over a mile from their smart detached home in Winchester Road.

X-rays showed that Henry had two fractures of the skull and doctors admitted him to Ward Four for observation. His mother Jenny recalls: 'He was still dizzy and had bad headaches. The following day he seemed a lot better and the doctors said they had thought about sending him home.'

But, instead of getting better, Henry's condition worsened over the Easter weekend.

By Saturday he was very ill, vomiting and sleeping a lot, and doctors warned his parents that, if he didn't improve, they would have to send him to the Queen's Medical Centre, in Nottingham, just as they had done with Kayley Desmond a few days before. It was a normal precaution for the more seriously ill youngster because Grantham hospital did not have the special facilities to care for critically ill children. The Q.M.C., less than an hour away by ambulance, had a reputation for being one of the finest hospitals in the country.

By Easter Sunday Henry was worse and started having fits. He had such a high temperature that a fan was placed by his side and he was put on a drip to keep him hydrated.

One of the nurses on duty remembered the moment when little Henry suffered a cardiac arrest. His pulse was high and he had the arrest soon afterwards. Henry was rushed to Nottingham by ambulance. His parents went too, desperately worried at what might happen. Jenny said: 'He was conscious, he knew I was his mum, and he seemed slightly improved when he got there. He had a scan that night and the doctors said they found a blood clot in his head which they reassured us wasn't a problem.'

Henry recovered so quickly that, by the following Friday, he was well enough to go home. For weeks Jenny and Eddie thought it was the fall that had nearly killed their son.

It had been a dreadful month for Ward Four as crisis after crisis hit each family.

In the world outside attention was focused on more pressing events. The Gulf War was over, though the fires in the desert were still burning. Tennis star Steffi Graf's father Peter had denied he was the father of a model's love child, the giant Intersun and Air Europe holiday firm had crashed, hitting 500,000 holidays, new Prime Minister John Major announced the end of the failed Poll Tax and Chancellor Norman Lamont had increased VAT to 17.5% in his Budget.

In America Eric Clapton's son Conor had plunged 750 feet to his death through a window in his skyscraper home and Mark Phillips was accused of fathering a secret love child in New Zealand, a claim he angrily denied.

But for more and more parents, nothing was more important to them than what was happening to their children at the Grantham and Kesteven General Hospital.

Without doubt the luckiest baby to survive on Ward Four was five-months-old Paul Crampton.

Much later, his escape from the brink of death was to provide the first conclusive evidence that what was happening was no cruel accident, no fluke of nature, no 'bad run'.

Blood samples would reveal that Paul, who was not diabetic, had a massive amount of insulin in his body; this had sent his sugar level plummeting. The human body needs sugar, mainly in the form of glucose, to feed the brain. In a normal, healthy child, the glucose level runs between 4 and 6 millimoles per litre of blood. The critical balance is controlled naturally by the body using insulin produced by the pancreas.

In the case of baby Paul, on three separate occasions in the space of eight days his insulin level suddenly, and with no apparent reason, soared so high that he collapsed with hypoglycemia, a critical lack of sugar in the body. His lips turned blue, he broke out in a sweat and rolled his eyes alarmingly. Luckily, doctors reacted quickly to the emergency and saved his life by pumping glucose into his body in such vast amounts that they countered the effects of the insulin.

Paul hadn't been seriously ill when he arrived on Ward Four on 20 March suffering from a heavy cold which had led to bronchiolitis, a severe chest infection. His mother, Kath, told other parents she only expected him to be there for a couple of days. In the ward's playroom, where her other two youngsters were letting off steam, she announced that Paul was doing so well he would soon be home.

For three days all was well, then, to everyone's surprise, other parents found Kath crying by the door to Cubicle Two where Paul had been lying but which was now empty. Sue Phillips, who was in the hospital with her twins Becky and Katie, tried to console Kath and asked what was wrong. Kath told her: 'It's Paul. He's taken a turn for the worse. They have got him in the treatment room.' Doctors were battling to save his life. Inside, Sue could see paediatrician Dr Nanayakkara and the blue uniforms of two nurses, one of them Nurse Allitt.

Sue said: 'I heard Bev Allitt say: "I think I know what's wrong with him. He is hypoglycemic." '

Paul was put on a glucose drip to counteract the shortage of sugar and quickly he showed signs of recovery.

Sue later said: 'When it was over, I thought how clever the nurse was to have realised what was wrong with him so quickly.'

Another nurse on the ward said: 'He had been fine apart from a slight temperature, which was reported, but then he arrested. Afterwards, when I saw him, he was surrounded by drips.'

It was several hours before Paul had recovered sufficiently to be wheeled back from the treatment room to his cubicle, attached to a resuscitaire. The previously healthy little boy suffered two more identical attacks in the next few days. Nobody could explain why Paul had suddenly become hypoglycemic. Kath and husband David, a chartered builder, were left feeling that the medical staff were confused.

'We asked questions, but the answers they gave us didn't seem to make sense. We felt the staff didn't know why Paul had become hypoglycemic,' recalled David.

Finally, Paul was transferred to Nottingham 'as a precaution'.

Sue Phillips recalled: 'His mum was in tears. One minute she had been told Paul was fine, then he was so ill. He had only gone into hospital for something simple and they only expected him to be there for a couple of days.'

Paul was taken to the Queen's Medical Centre in Nottingham where he, like the others, made a full recovery.

Doctors took a sample of his blood to send away to a laboratory at Cardiff University for analysis, hoping for a clue that might explain what had happened to him. The results were to be shocking.

4. Becky and Katie

Twins Becky and Katie Phillips, who had been kept in hospital for observation after their premature birth, put on weight quickly and finally came home on 4 March when they were almost five weeks old. It was an exciting time and friends and neighbours poured in to welcome the girls.

Sue brought them home in identical pink and white dresses, pink cardigans and frilly white socks.

They were already showing their individual characters – Katie was always 'a bit faddy', as Sue put it, often playing up a little, while Becky was always very calm and placid. They wondered if it would continue that way for the rest of their lives.

As they peered dotingly at the two, near-identical babies both asleep in their separate cots in the new back-bedroom nursery, proud father Peter remembers how he turned, smiling, to Sue and beamed: 'They're beautiful. They're going to break a few hearts when they grow up.'

But hearts were to be broken much quicker than that.

Just nine days later Katie went back into hospital. She had had a tummy bug and, after twenty-four hours, the family doctor decided she should go into hospital to be monitored, just as a precaution, though he suspected it was nothing more than gastro-enteritis.

As she walked on to Ward Four Sue recognised Nurse Beverley Allitt whom she hadn't seen since they were students together.

Sue recalls: 'I spotted her straight away. I hadn't seen her for about five years, since we were at the Grantham College of Further Education together. I didn't know her really well and I didn't know she had actually become a nurse until I saw her there in the ward.

'She wore two badges – one for the Lincolnshire School of Nursing and the other for the Royal College of Nursing.

'But, while I recognised her, she made no sign of acknowledging that she knew me. She just carried on working and I was more worried about seeing how Katie was. I didn't even stop to speak to her.'

Sue also recognised Sister Barbara Barker who had been on the ward so long that she had nursed Sue herself twice as a child – once, at age six, when she swallowed a chocolate Brazil nut which had stuck in her throat and another, at the age of nine, when she had an 'abscess on my bum the size of an orange'.

Katie was in the hospital for four days and was then allowed home. Then both girls were sick and the doctor sent them both back to Ward Four.

Two days later brother James, then aged four, went down with a bug and he, too, was admitted, so that all three of the Phillips's children were patients in the same children's ward.

On her visits to the children Sue again saw Nurse Allitt several times, always busy working, but, again, the two women didn't speak or acknowledge each other. Twice Sue noticed the chubby, blonde nurse attending to either her twins or to James, but nothing was said.

After five days the twins were sent home but doctors still couldn't explain why they had been ill. James came home two days later. Then Becky became ill again; frantic, Sue was getting to the end of her tether.

She said: 'I took her back to the hospital. What else could I do? She was throwing up all over the place.' It was 'projectile vomiting' which, Sue said, two-month-old Becky could send flying almost three feet.

'But they made me feel paranoid. The doctor who came said: "What is it this time, Mrs Phillips?"

'I suppose you couldn't blame him, but Becky was ill and there was nothing I could do about that.'

Doctors finally discovered that the type of milk being given to the twins was the cause of the problem. The hospital used ready-mixed baby's milk but Sue mixed her own from powder.

Relieved that the problem had been identified Sue went to bring Becky home from the hospital on 4 April and was pleased to hear that she had just been fed. She was surprised, however, when Nurse Allitt told her that it was not a good idea for

Becky to go home, and tried to persuade her to leave her in the hospital.

Sue said: 'She didn't want her to go home. She said she didn't like the look of her and thought she should stay in. The Sister on duty had a good look at her and said Becky seemed fine to her and told me I could take her. The decision seemed to annoy Nurse Allitt.'

Sue, happy to have the babies together again at home, put them both straight into their baby chairs in the lounge so they could sleep and, with Peter still not home from work, she sat down in front of the TV at 7.30pm to enjoy the start of her favourite programme, 'EastEnders'.

She thought the nightmare was finally over. But it was only about to begin.

Becky started to scream. Sue rushed over to pick her up. Surely she couldn't need feeding again so soon? She must be still full from the hospital.

Sue said: 'The screams stopped as I held her. I was looking into her face, watching for a sign of what might be wrong, when I saw her eyeballs just drop down to the bottom of their sockets. I was just looking at the whites of her eyes, nothing more.

'I thought I was seeing things. It was awful and I didn't know what it was. Then, just as quickly as it had started, it was over.

'I had to feed Katie and James was playing up, then Katie started crying and I was literally tearing my hair out wondering what to do next when Peter finally came home from work at about 8 o'clock.'

Sue was holding Becky, who was crying in her

arms, and Peter took her. He was still holding her when she let out another awful scream. She was not yet nine weeks old but the sound was ear-piercing.

Sue said: 'It was as if someone had stabbed her. It was a pitiful scream that will haunt me for the rest of my life.'

Frantically they wondered what could be wrong with her. Sue thought it must be wind. Peter said: 'That's the cry of a kid in pain.'

Sue remembers snapping back at him: 'Don't be ridiculous. She only came out of hospital four hours ago.'

Peter suggested calling the doctor but Sue would have none of it because she didn't want to be seen as a nuisance. She said afterwards: 'I should have let him. I should have listened to him then, but I didn't.'

She convinced herself that Becky must have wind because, if it had been anything more serious, the hospital would have found it.

They put Jamie to bed and Katie fell asleep downstairs. Becky was awake but quiet and seemed happy.

Then at 10.30pm it started again. She was screaming and crying and contorting her face. 'She was doing weird things with her face, twisting it up,' said Sue. 'It looked as though she could be having an epileptic fit. We began to panic because we didn't know what was happening.'

Peter telephoned for the emergency doctor and a local GP arrived at about 11pm. He watched

Becky's face contort and heard her screams. It could be severe colic, he thought, and suggested feeding her. He had another patient to see and he would return. Sue gave Becky a feed and, when the GP came back, he winded her. She seemed better. Yes, it must be colic. Becky fell sound asleep.

Reassuring the now exhausted couple, he told them the best advice to them was to go to bed and get some sleep themselves.

At 2.30am Katie awoke as expected, ready for her night feed. Sue noticed that Becky, too, was stirring. She picked Becky up in her arms, holding her as always, with her bottom in one hand and the other hand supporting her head, when Becky suddenly went into spasms again. Her little face contorted and her eyes started rolling. It didn't last long and then she dropped off to sleep again.

'We were so worried, we took her into our double bed and put her between us, thinking that she would wake up in another quarter of an hour for her feed anyway.'

Becky normally breathed quite heavily when she slept. You could hear the little sighs made by her breathing across the room. Peter was to hear first the awful sound of silence. As he looked down at Becky, he was filled with a sense of panic and shouted: 'She's stopped breathing.'

Sue, still half asleep, told him: 'Oh, Peter! Don't be silly.'

But, as she turned, she could see her husband holding Becky in his arms and trying to blow into her mouth. She was lying limp and lifeless, like a rag doll. He began massaging her chest, battling to get her back to life, and shouting through tears for Sue to phone for an ambulance.

They didn't wait for the ambulance to arrive. They raced instead to their car and drove to the hospital, half a mile away, dashing straight up to the doors of the Accident and Emergency Department where they pressed the emergency doorbell, virtually kicking the door down. In the middle of the night the door was locked for security reasons. A nurse quickly opened it and Sue, who had been holding Becky, thrust the limp, lifeless body into her arms.

The nurse ran off shouting: 'Resus. Resus.'

But it was too late. Becky was already dead. She had died at home as she lay in their bed after her last outburst of screams. The hospital did what it could but Becky was pronounced dead at 3.55am on 5 April 1991.

Sue remembers that every nurse at the hospital seemed to be in tears and doctors couldn't explain what had happened. Genuine words of love and comfort poured out from the staff.

But why had she died so soon after being discharged from hospital? Becky had been in hospital for two days and been home less than twelve hours. Now she was dead, without any apparent reason. Sue's thoughts flashed back to the moment when Nurse Allitt had said she should not take her daughter home.

Now she turned to the doctor on duty and

demanded: 'I want to know what has killed Becky.' But he couldn't tell her.

He feared it could be meningitis. And Sue was sent hurrying back home to bring in Katie for urgent checks. Whatever it was that had tragically killed Becky might strike down her twin sister too. Katie was taken back to Ward Four for observation.

It was to be her turn next. Later that same day Katie was fighting for her own little life.

It was 7.30am when Nurse Bev Allitt arrived to start the day shift on Ward Four. Becky had been dead less than five hours and now she was told to monitor her tiny twin sister, Katie.

Sue Phillips remembers that, from the start of that day, the nurse was a different person. For the first time she spoke to Sue. Her words, warm and comforting, still stick clear in Sue's memory. Nurse Allitt whispered: 'I am ever so sorry, Sue, that Becky died. But don't worry about Katie. She will be fine.'

She hadn't spoken to Sue for three years and now she was genuinely concerned. It was the first indication to Sue that Nurse Allitt even remembered her.

Sue couldn't control her anger at the hospital and snapped back: 'I find it very strange how the staff on this ward have treated me while I have been bringing my babies in here, and now that Becky has died it's all so different.'

It was the forgivable outburst of an angry mother whose little baby had just died. Calmly defusing the

confrontation, the nurse told her softly: 'That sometimes happens when someone dies, Sue.'

The police arrived – called by the hospital as a
matter of routine to make enquiries into Becky's
'sudden death'. Peter, who had broken down,
crying uncontrollably when he was told Becky was
dead, still couldn't bring himself to identify Becky's
body, and the job was left to Sue. She was led
quietly into a room where she identified the body
of Becky Grace Phillips to the waiting police
officer. Her baby, born just nine weeks earlier, was
at peace, looking as though she was fast asleep.

For strength, she returned to Ward Four where
Katie was perfectly healthy. She was in the hospital
just as a precaution, to be monitored, they said,
after the death of Becky.

Desperately tired, they wanted to go home for a
break at lunchtime. It had been an awful night
and Katie was asleep. Sue remembers Nurse Allitt
saying: 'You go. I will look after her. She will be all
right with me.' They had been home just half an
hour when the phone rang. A man's voice from the
hospital told Peter that Katie was having trouble
breathing – and they wanted one of them to go
back to the hospital.

It didn't sound like an emergency. Sue and her
father had already steeled themselves emotionally
to go to the undertakers that afternoon to begin
arranging Becky's funeral, a job they were dreading but one that had to be done. Peter decided to
return to the hospital alone to see Katie. When he
arrived he realised it was more serious than he'd

expected. Katie had been placed on a resuscitaire, to help her breathing, and Sister Jean Saville was caring for her.

Sister Saville, who was forty-nine and one of the most experienced nurses in the hospital, had brought up two children herself and had a reputation for dedication and skill. She stayed until 10pm looking after Katie.

As Peter waited the hospital's chaplain, the Rev. Ian Shelton, approached him. He suggested to Peter that, in the circumstances, it might be advisable for Katie to be baptised. He thought it should be done there and then, where she lay in the cubicle on Ward Four. When Peter agreed, he went off to the chapel to change into his robes and returned to baptise Katie. By the time Sue arrived, unaware of the scare, the short service was already over.

All the next day Katie recovered, still linked to the resuscitaire. She also had a special Apnia Alarm, fitted to her chest, that would sound if she stopped breathing. It went off several times on false alarms, triggered because Katie was sleeping so quietly it couldn't detect the minute movements of her breathing. It terrified Sue and the nurses although, deep down, Sue was comforted by the thought that the hospital was taking no chances.

Nurse Bev Allitt was on duty that Saturday and again nursed Katie all day on a one-to-one basis. Katie seemed to be 'her baby'.

Relieved, Sue and Peter popped upstairs for a snack with the chaplain, leaving Nurse Allitt and another young nurse to look after her.

They were just returning to the ward when they heard the sound of a woman's voice shouting: 'Resus. Resus.' It was Nurse Allitt calling for help because Katie had stopped breathing.

Peter said: 'When we got down to the ward we saw a nurse running across the end of the corridor, clutching Katie to her chest, shouting. We hadn't been gone that long and I couldn't believe it was happening again.'

Doctors and nurses poured into the treatment room and began the battle to save her little life. Their efforts were rewarded when finally, after just a few minutes, they managed to bring Katie round.

Peter said: 'We were just so thankful that she made it. Neither of us could have taken losing her too. When we knew she was all right we were just grateful to Bev. She'd acted so quickly that she had saved Katie's life.'

Sue asked Nurse Allitt what had happened and she told her she had seen nothing like it before.

Nurse Allitt went home at the end of her shift, leaving Sue and Peter to battle with a mixture of emotions, partly grief over Becky and partly worry over Katie.

The Rev. Shelton, who arrived to comfort them, took the brunt of Peter's anger and grief. 'Some God you've got,' snapped Peter. 'I don't think your God's very fair, do you?'

The Rev. Shelton replied: 'Not very fair at all, Peter.'

Peter said: 'Isn't He satisfied with all He's got?

He's got Becky and now He's taking Katie, too.'

Later, bound by a bond forged amongst the heartbreak of Ward Four, the Rev. Shelton was to become a trusted friend and Katie's godfather.

Still battered by events, Sue found comfort in the reassuring presence of her new friend; Nurse Allitt was, by now, always referred to as 'Bev'. She was always there, assigned almost like a fixture to Katie's bedside. She was hard to talk to, said Sue, not one who gushed with words or feelings but, during her eight-hour shifts, they talked a lot.

Worried Sue was anxious when doctors took away Katie for a lumbar puncture, to test for meningitis, and Bev told her: 'Don't worry, I will be with her all the time.'

During the night Katie was 'perking up wonderfully'.

But, three days later, Katie took a sudden and massive turn for the worse. She'd seemed to be fine but then, suddenly, she stopped breathing. The hospital's 'crash team' rushed again to help. Dr Nanayakkara and Sister Saville jointly led the battle to save her life. The Rev. Shelton, who was on the ward, joined in too by running for extra equipment.

Peter remembers Nurse Allitt telling him Katie was in a bad way. He saw Dr Nanayakkara, who had put on green overalls, with Katie's head in his hands, cradling her face. He told them he couldn't understand what had happened because he said he had never seen anything like it. This time, he said, Katie was so poorly that he warned them he might have to call for the flying squad to rush her to Nottingham City Hospital.

As they waited Sue and Peter were told that the doctors and nurses were trying to bring her back. She was 'dead' but they were using every piece of equipment – oxygen bags, electric paddles – desperately willing her back to life.

Sister Saville stayed at the machine, refusing to give in, just hoping, trying for that little bit longer, waiting for a miracle. Sue believes that Katie was dead for an incredible thirty-two minutes. Certainly, long, long after Katie 'died', Sister Saville spotted a flicker of life. Then another one, and another. Her shouts signalled that Katie, incredibly, was coming back to life.

Out of heartbreak there was sudden joy. Peter and Sue hugged each other, tears rolling down their cheeks. Perhaps God had a heart after all, thought Peter.

'We're not religious but we went to the hospital chapel to ask God to give her strength to see her through,' he said.

The flying squad, with police escort, raced to Nottingham with Katie, her parents trying to keep up behind them in their own car.

Sue and Peter stayed with Katie, maintaining a vigil of love and hope at her bedside, refusing to leave her. The only break they were forced to make was to return to Grantham for Becky's funeral.

Life or, rather, death had to go on.

The whole community was overwhelmed with

compassion for Sue and Peter as Becky was buried at St John's Church, Manthorpe, on Wednesday, 10 April. The church was packed with relatives and friends, and nurses from the hospital. Lovingly, Sue said her farewells in the chapel of rest where she gently placed two of Becky's little teddy bears and a rose in the coffin.

They were told they couldn't have a hearse because Becky's tiny white coffin was too small to rest in the back of a vehicle which had been designed for much bigger coffins. Instead, they had a huge black limousine in which Sue and Peter could sit in the back; Becky's white coffin was placed in front of them on a seat.

They chose a wreath in the shape of a heart, with white and pink carnations and red roses. Their card read: 'In loving memory of our beautiful baby, Becky. We will love you for ever.' It was signed: 'Mum, Dad, James, Katie, Nicola and Emma'.

There were about thirty people in the quiet village church on the outskirts of Grantham. Mourners included some of the nurses from the hospital's Accident and Emergency department who had shared their moment of horror as they had burst in, in the middle of the night, with Becky's body in their arms. Sue's new-found friend Bev Allitt was not amongst them.

Sue and Peter were told that Becky had officially died from Infant Death Syndrome – a 'cot death' - and Sue couldn't hide her feelings of amazement. How could they say that Becky had died of cot death when she had watched her eyes rolling round in her head and heard her screams? Surely, 'cot death' babies died without warning in their sleep?

But there wasn't time to question, or challenge, the findings of the doctors because they had to drive straight from the funeral back to Katie's bedside. It was Katie who needed them now. At the hospital, nurses and doctors couldn't have been kinder, providing them with a family room with all facilities, including a TV, so they could be near Katie.

She was still very poorly and continued to have fits. Peter and Sue almost feared she might be ill because of a psychological bonding that exists between twins; in some strange way, could Becky be calling Katie to follow her to the grave?

But Katie was a battler and, slowly, she began showing signs of recovery. She was gurgling, feeding, occasionally smiling. At last they really could start thinking of a future for their little girl. Becky had died but Katie was alive and kicking.

Twelve days after Becky had died Katie was well enough to leave Nottingham where she had recovered so wonderfully well. She wasn't strong enough to go home, however. Instead, Sue and Peter were told she would be returned to Ward Four at the Grantham and Kesteven Hospital.

5. A Run of Bad Luck

Ward Four had always been a happy place; morale had been high and nurses had enjoyed working there. This was a ward where the real reward was seeing sick children get better and then go home. The worst of the emergency cases were transferred to bigger hospitals in Nottingham, thirty miles to the west, and in Grantham nurses would tell new members of staff that 'nothing much happens on the children's ward'.

It was a friendly hospital where people knew each other, where patients knew nurses because they'd probably gone to school together, or knew their families.

But now, after the deaths of Liam Taylor, Timothy Hardwick, then Becky Phillips, some of the younger nurses were finding it hard to cope with the increasing number of emergencies. More and more children suffered cardiac arrests, respiratory failures and fits. To them, it was still a run of 'bad luck' and there remained no real suspicion, no nagging question that anything untoward was happening.

Five-year-old Bradley Gibson was the next victim of Ward Four.

Blonde-haired Bradley, who had gone into hospital suffering from pneumonia, suffered a massive, unexplained heart attack. His heart stopped beating for thirty-two minutes as 'crash team' nurses and doctors battled for his little life, refusing to give up as the minutes ticked away. Then, quite miraculously, there was a flicker of hope, the sign of a heartbeat and Bradley was brought back to life.

His parents, self-employed builder Stephen and wife Judith, were so overjoyed that their son had been saved that they went to their local newspaper publicly to praise the hospital, doctors and nurses. The story of how he survived made the front page of the local *Grantham Journal* with the headline: 'Our Miracle.' Three national newspapers followed up the story of Bradley's great escape and it featured also on four television stations.

Mother Judith told reporters: 'It's a miracle. There is just no other word for it. If it were not for the crash team at Grantham Hospital, he would not be here today.' She added: 'We never really gave up hope. We did some serious talking and were prepared for the worst but I knew he would make it. I suppose it's maternal instinct.'

The cause of his heart attack, however, was 'baffling' doctors, Judith said. She couldn't explain why her son had suddenly collapsed. She could only say: 'He's had a number of tests. He's been on drips and ventilators and had all sorts of needles put into him, but they don't seem to know why he had the heart attack or how he recovered so quickly.'

Within three weeks Bradley was well enough to be back at his desk at the Gonerby Hill Foot Primary School, apparently unaffected by his experience.

His mother Judith, an intelligent, articulate woman, would much later become the backbone of a Parents' Support Group, formed to unite all the families of Ward Four children. Among them was Belinda King who worked as a nurse on a different ward at the same hospital. Even she was not to be spared; her month-old baby son, Christopher, was the next to follow, though he too survived.

The toll of children continued and staff were now reeling from the scale of it. Some were beginning to suspect that something was wrong, alerted only by the fact that there had never been so many emergencies, rather than by any medical proof.

One young nurse remembers: 'We weren't prepared for what was happening. You'd go off duty at 9pm, leaving one of the children perfectly OK, then, when you went in the next morning at 7.30am, you'd be told so and so had suffered a heart attack and been transferred to Nottingham. When it happened once or twice you didn't think much about it, but it was happening more and more . . .'

Becky's death had come as a blow to them. One of the nurses said: 'I remember her going home. She was a lovely little thing. She was perfectly OK when she went home in the afternoon. The next day when I went on duty I said good morning to one of the staff nurses. She said: "It's not a good morning, it's just morning." I said why, and she said Becky had been brought into casualty dead on arrival. I couldn't believe it. It was so ridiculous.'

Little more than seven weeks had passed since the death of baby Liam Taylor, the first victim, but by now the emergency crash team were frequent visitors to the ward. They had brought several children back from the brink of death.

Two-month-old Christopher Peasgood was to be the next. He'd been born at the hospital on 17 February, weighing 6lbs. His birth had been a special blessing to mother Creswen and father Mick who had lost their ten-month-old daughter, Michelle, in a cot-death tragedy two years earlier.

There had been the worry that Christopher could die, just like Michelle, in his sleep, but, as the weeks went by, his parents began to feel that everything was going to be all right. At seven weeks Christopher developed a nasty cough, lost his appetite and began to struggle for breath. Antibiotics had no effect so, on Friday, 13 April, Christopher was admitted to Ward Four.

After Michelle's death Creswen and Mick were taking no chances. 'We insisted they took him in,' recalls Creswen.

Specialist Dr Nanayyakara was quick to reassure Christopher's mother. Her baby was suffering from bronchiolitis, but little children were durable and, given a couple of days, he would be fine. They put an oxygen mask on Christopher's face, which seemed to help him breathe, and Creswen and Mick were content enough to go home that night, leaving their son in the care of Ward Four.

When they returned the next day, Christopher was inside an oxygen tent which they were told was nothing to worry about, a routine measure because he wouldn't settle with the mask over his face.

From time to time Nurse Allitt popped in and out of Cubicle Two to check on Christopher who was being fed by tubes. When it was time to give him some medicine Creswen called in Nurse Allitt; she remembers the nurse telling her: 'Why don't you go for a drink, and a cigarette? He's all right. He's fast asleep. Don't worry, I'll look after him.'

Reassured, Creswen and Mick took a break. They were only gone ten minutes but, as they returned, Creswen saw the 'crash team' rushing to the ward. Instinctively, she knew it was Christopher. 'Something clicked in my brain and I suddenly thought: "He's dead."'

The doctors and nurses were already beside Christopher's bed when she looked inside Cubicle Two.

It was a horrifying sight, she said. 'The oxygen tent had gone and he was laid on the bed, totally blue. His face was the colour of a nurse's blue hat. They were trying to bring him back, but I thought he had gone. I knew what a dead baby looked like because I'd carried Michelle to the ambulance in my arms.' The realisation of what was happening to her little boy was just too much for Creswen, who became hysterical, screaming to doctors: 'Bring him back – don't you dare let him die.'

It was Nurse Allitt who led Creswen from the room. Creswen remembers the nurse trying to comfort her. 'She said, "Come on, he's all right, they're bringing him back. We'll get you a cup of tea." She took me to the tea room with her arm around me and she seemed ever so concerned.

'They carried Christopher out, he was just limp, and they took him to the treatment room. Nurse Allitt came into the parents room where she told us: "Don't worry, he'll be all right. He's in the best hands." '

By mid-afternoon Christopher's condition had stabilised and doctors said they were sure he was going to be all right. Creswen asked what had caused her son to stop breathing; she was told that sometimes children suffering from bronchiolitis had mild cardiac arrests. 'We accepted what they told us.'

But then, suddenly at 8pm, it happened again. Christopher suffered another cardiac arrest and, this time, it was worse. The 'crash team' was doing its best, but Creswen feared it would not be enough. 'We really thought we were losing him. The doctors and nurses mentioned we ought to get him christened, and we agreed.'

Creswen would never forget the scene. Hospital chaplain, the Rev. Shelton, was summoned again to the ward. A gentle man with a strong sense of faith, he had become a frequent visitor to the ward. The number of calls from the hospital had been unusually high. In the space of a few months he had been summoned nine times to comfort parents on the ward, mostly in the middle of the night. Other ministers had answered two other calls.

He had tried to console Chris and Joanne Taylor after Liam's death, and had conducted the funeral service at the crematorium on 1 March. He had also shared Peter and Sue Phillips's grief and had buried Becky in his churchyard at Manthorpe on 10 April.

Now here he was, four days later, baptising little Christopher whose life was also threatened. It was all over in a matter of minutes. There was no time to choose godparents, only time to pray that Christopher had the strength to pull through. 'Christopher was on the machines and there were tubes everywhere. We gave him the name Christopher William Stephen Peasgood.

'The minister took two photographs of him just lying there. It was all so weird.'

It was decided that Christopher would have to be transferred to the Queen's Medical Centre in Nottingham, but he was so ill that they were warned he might not survive the journey.

It was their decision but Creswen asked one of the nurses what she ought to do. 'She told us, "Move him." I'll never forget her words. We thought we had nothing to lose.'

There wasn't room in the ambulance for Creswen and Mick. Convinced they were going to lose their second child they drove to Nottingham, stopping off en route to collect two friends to help them face the battle that lay ahead. When they arrived at the intensive care unit, however, they found that Christopher had made a remarkable recovery. 'He'd had two arrests at Grantham and we'd been told he would die unless he got to a respirator, but when we got to Nottingham the doctor was full of hope. The doctor there said: "He's not going to die, he's perfectly all right." '

Creswen only had to look at Christopher to be convinced he would pull through. 'He was lying there on a huge bed big enough for a fourteen-year-old, and he was screaming his lungs out. He was hungry. I fed him a bottle and I couldn't believe it. We'd lost Michelle, we'd expected the worst, and there he was safe and well.'

Three days later Christopher had recovered sufficiently to go home. In the weeks that followed Creswen would wonder at her baby's lucky escape, and ask herself: 'Why was he dying one minute and OK the next?'

On the day Creswen took her baby home from the Queen's Medical Centre, still counting her blessings, another baby, seven-week-old Patrick Elstone, was admitted to Ward Four. Like most of the parents, Hazel and Robert weren't unduly worried about their baby's arrival at the hospital.

Patrick and his identical twin brother, Anthony, were their first children. There had been no problems until Patrick developed a cold and stopped taking his feed; at this point the family doctor had suggested a check-up at the hospital. It was a routine precaution, simply a case of keeping him under observation.

But within forty-eight hours Patrick nearly died too. He stopped breathing without warning and was so ill that he, too, was baptised as he lay fighting for his life.

At first there had been no cause for alarm. Robert and Hazel spent two-and-a-half hours by their son's bedside, then went home to put twin brother, Anthony, to bed at 9pm, satisfied that little Patrick couldn't have been in better hands.

They sat by his side throughout the next day as Patrick lay in a maternity cot, seemingly doing so well that it wasn't going to be necessary to put him on a drip. On the third day Patrick's temperature went up slightly and staff suggested Hazel should take Anthony to the doctor for a check-up, in case he was suffering from something too.

Hazel left the ward at 2pm when Patrick was laughing in his cot, kicking and cooing.

But when her taxi-driver husband Robert phoned the hospital at 8pm he was told by a nurse that staff had been trying to reach them. Patrick had been 'sort of playing up', and the nurse said they should go straight to the ward.

Hazel bundled Anthony into her arms and the couple dashed to the hospital, a mile from their terraced cottage near the town's railway station. 'As soon as we got in we got the shock of our lives. We sat there and a nurse called Mary told us Patrick had stopped breathing at 8pm.

'I said: "What's happening, will he live?" She

said: "I cannot tell you one way or the other. We're hoping to have him moved to Nottingham." I just broke down in tears.'

Sue Phillips had been sitting with Katie near the cubicle where Patrick lay. She remembered watching Nurse Allitt come from Cubicle Six carrying Patrick in her arms, shouting that he had stopped breathing. She'd just gone in to check him, she had said, and found him already turning blue. The night sister, Jean Saville, helped, and Patrick quickly began breathing again.

Upstairs, in the canteen, Hazel and Robert met Sue and Peter Phillips, who, as much as anyone, knew what the Elstones were going through. They had already lost Becky and were still waiting for Katie to be allowed home. Hazel knew Sue from the ante-natal classes where they had met and chatted about the coming birth of their babies; they had both given birth to twins.

Sue tried to tell Hazel not to worry. She told them that the doctors were very good at Nottingham and she was sure Patrick would recover.

It was 9pm before Hazel and Robert were taken to see Patrick. All they wanted to know was whether he would live or die.

Hazel recalls: 'I was crying, and saying, would he be all right? They were saying they didn't know.' She said specialist Dr Nelson Porter couldn't tell her what was wrong with him.

Hazel's last sight of her baby before he left for the Queen's Medical Centre would live in her memory forever. She had asked if she could see him, but one of the nurses replied: 'Are you sure you want to . . .?'

Hazel thought she would be able to pick up Patrick and cuddle him. Instead she recalls: 'When I looked through the door I was stunned. He had no clothes on, just a little white cap on his head.

'There was a doctor holding a tube down his throat to help him breathe, and Patrick was fighting it. I looked at his little face but he had no colour at all. He was as white as a sheet.

'I couldn't believe it. When I had left him he had been playing, laughing and cooing. It wasn't the same child in there. I just looked at him and said: "Oh my God – look at his colour." The Sister dropped a blanket over him. Robert and I were just hanging on to each other.'

There was so much equipment in the ambulance carrying Patrick to Nottingham that there wasn't room for Hazel and Robert.

When they arrived at the intensive care unit, a nurse quietly asked them if they wanted a priest to be called to baptise their son. If he was to die, then the Elstones felt he should be christened before it was too late. At 1am the priest arrived and, when he realised that Patrick was a twin, and his brother was there, he decided to baptise both of them in the middle of the night. A nurse they didn't know stood in as a godparent, though Hazel and Robert were in such a daze they never even asked her name. Patrick lay there surrounded by tubes, wires and monitors, limp, barely alive, with his eyes closed.

Staff advised the Elstones to get some sleep but, try as she might, Hazel couldn't rest.

At 7am a nurse delivered good news. Patrick seemed a little better and was making progress. For two days he continued to get better.

Then, just as the doctors were beginning to talk of transferring him back to Grantham, Patrick suffered his first fit. Robert was holding his hand when he began to twitch and shake. 'Robert asked the doctor what was happening. The doctor told us it was a fit and, after that, he started having fits every time he opened his eyes. They'd last about a minute each time.'

It's a strange medical phenomenon that twins often share the same ailments, even feeling the same pain, and after Patrick had fought for his little life, twin brother Anthony also fell ill. Anthony, too, was admitted to Queen's. The doctors diagnosed diarrhoea, but said it could be trauma triggered by being parted from his identical brother.

Hazel remembers: 'Anthony was screaming a lot and they thought it was because Patrick was ill. He was missing him so much he was playing up.'

Eventually, both children were discharged and, once he was home, Patrick's fits stopped altogether. Hazel often wondered what had happened to cause her son to stop breathing on Ward Four. Later, she would take Patrick back to Grantham and Kesteven Hospital for a check-up and find out more about the night her baby almost died. She would discover that his heart had stopped beating not once, but twice, in the space of four hours. But even then nobody could tell Hazel Elstone why it had happened.

At the Queen's Medical Centre in Nottingham questions were being asked about the high number of seriously ill children who were being transferred from Ward Four at Grantham.

A number of doctors expressed concern. Five children had been rushed thirty miles along the A52 from Grantham to Nottingham for specialist care in less than two months – normally the number they would expect in an entire year. All of them had made a recovery but the doctors at the QMC were sufficiently worried to approach a senior consultant.

What on earth, they wanted to know, could be happening?

6. Claire – 'Crikey, Not Another One'

It took the death of Claire Peck finally to bring detectives onto Ward Four at the Grantham and Kesteven Hospital.

Three children, Liam Taylor, Timothy Hardwick and Becky Phillips had died. Eight other youngsters, Kayley Desmond, Paul Crampton, Bradley Gibson, Henry Chan, Katie Phillips, Christopher Peasgood, Christopher King and Patrick Elstone had been a whisker away from losing their lives; yet Ward Four still remained open.

But after the death of Claire – child number twelve in the catalogue of tragedy – attitudes were to change.

It had been a routine case. Claire was an only child, blonde-haired, bright eyed, just beginning to talk and find her feet. She was fifteen months old and asthmatic.

Her life hadn't been in real danger when she was admitted to the ward on the afternoon of 22 April. Claire was gasping for breath as Sue and David Peck drove fifteen miles to the hospital from their home on the outskirts of Newark, but the family doctor had said twenty-four hours would bring a remarkable recovery in her condition.

Within four hours Claire Peck was dead. Sue would always remember the specialist sitting bewildered, with his head in his hands, shattered from the effort of trying to save Claire, telling her it should not have happened. At the time Sue didn't understand what he meant.

Hairdresser Sue Peck, a friendly girl with a ready grin, had been married four years when Claire was born in the maternity ward at Grantham; she weighed 6lbs 8ozs. She was surrounded by love, adored by David and their relatives and friends who would make a habit of calling in just to catch sight of her smile.

When Claire was fifteen months old she suddenly started to wheeze at night and Sue and David were plunged into despair. She would cough for hours on end, unable to sleep. The doctor diagnosed bronchiolitis and prescribed a Ventolin inhaler, saying it was too soon to know whether Claire was going to be asthmatic. By 18 April the wheezing was no better and the doctor declared she would have to be admitted to hospital.

On Ward Four nurses placed Claire on a nebuliser to clear her airways. Within half an hour she was 100% better. Claire remained in hospital until 20 April, improving hour by hour. A doctor admitted that Claire was asthmatic 'to a slight degree', and sent her home, advising Sue to administer a course of Ventolin syrup and use the inhaler when necessary.

The following morning, 21 April, was a beautiful spring day. It was to be Claire's last full day at home, the day before she died, and Sue and David would remember it vividly. They took Claire for a walk in the country, carrying her some of the time, then watching her proudly as she tried to put one step in front of the other and walk.

They called in to see Sue's grandma, popped in at her brother's home, then went home to put Claire in the bath before bed. 'It had been a beautiful day, lovely and warm, and we had had a wonderful time together.'

Claire woke coughing at 1.45am and, when Sue phoned the doctor, he told her to administer twenty puffs of Ventolin and some syrup. Claire recovered, played with her toys for an hour, then fell asleep. At 4.30am David left for work. At 6.15am Sue woke to the sound of her little girl coughing once more. The doctor was at the house before 8am, with a portable nebuliser, returning a second time at 2pm, but the second time it made no difference and, when David took Claire to the surgery, the doctor said she would have to go back to the hospital straightaway.

David left the surgery with the doctor's voice ringing in his ears. 'He said that, in twenty-four hours, there would be a remarkable recovery in her condition.' Sue climbed behind the wheel of the couple's Vauxhall Astra for the journey to Ward Four. David cradled Claire in his arms in the back seat as she gasped for air.

Sue was desperately worried. 'I was frightened she

would die. I thought perhaps we should have gone to the hospital earlier than we had. She was trying to cry, but she couldn't get enough air to make any noise. She was just moaning, ruttling and gasping.'

In Ward Four Claire was placed on a nebuliser, but it made no difference and, when they tried to take her blood pressure, Claire's arm turned blue. They attached a heart monitor but the machine didn't work.

Nurse Allitt had been sitting at a desk as Claire arrived. Sue recognised her from the previous visit and remembered her as being very unfriendly towards them.

'I had run out of nappies and Nurse Allitt had brought them in. She didn't say anything when she gave them to me, she just slammed them down on the table and walked off. All the other nurses had made a habit of picking Claire up, playing with her and, when she was in the bath, they would come into the bathroom and splash her and tip water over her head. Claire loved it. But once, when she was in the bath, Nurse Allitt came past and just walked by, and ignored Claire. I remember clear as day turning to Claire, and saying: "We don't care if she doesn't want to talk to you, sweetheart . . ." so when I saw her that day I knew I didn't like her.'

Sue finds it hard to think of Claire's final few hours without shedding a tear. Time has done little to ease the pain. The nightmare began with specialist Dr Nelson Porter announcing that he proposed to insert a tube down Claire's throat to open her airways. Sue couldn't bear the prospect of watching and handed Claire to a nurse. It was 4.55pm, and Sue and David were told the routine procedure wouldn't take too long. They left Claire in the treatment room and walked to the TV lounge to wait for news.

The medical team prepared to give Claire a new drug which had to be administered in such precise amounts that the duty doctor went in search of paediatrician Dr Porter for guidance, leaving Claire in the treatment room with Nurse Allitt and another nurse.

While he was gone Nurse Allitt agreed to stay while her colleague went down the corridor to tell Claire's parents what was happening. Within seconds – even before the nurse had time to reach David and Sue Peck – Beverley Allitt cried for help from the room. She was shouting 'Arrest, Arrest.'

And when other nurses and doctors dashed to Claire's bedside they found she had suffered a respiratory failure and was having trouble breathing. They gave her oxygen and Claire recovered quickly.

David and Sue were on the verge of going to see what had happened when the ward sister, Barbara Barker, appeared. The news wasn't good – the medical team was still working to improve her condition.

Claire's parents asked only one question: 'Is she going to be all right . . .?' The Sister didn't say yes, and she didn't say no. Instead, she told David and Sue she hoped Claire would recover. It wasn't the answer Claire's parents had wanted to hear.

Sue recalls: 'We were worried when she gave us our answer. Up to then we had never really imagined that she was going to die. My mum and dad had arrived by this time and they had expected to see Claire recovered.'

As the fight to save Claire continued in the treatment room Sue, David and her parents paced the TV lounge, desperately anxious for reassurance. They lost all track of time.

In the treatment room Dr Porter finally administered the drug himself and left Claire in the care of Nurse Allitt who was accompanied for a short period by another nurse until the Ward Sister told them it didn't need two of them there. The second nurse had only just left when Nurse Allitt cried out again from the treatment room: 'Arrest.' This time Claire had suffered cardiac failure.

Dr Porter and Sister Barker had just asked Claire's parents if they would like to see their little girl. Her condition was now stable and they had succeeded in stemming the attack with drugs, they told them. If Claire remained stable for the next twenty minutes then she would be transferred to the Queen's Medical Centre in Nottingham where facilities were better.

David and Sue were on their way to the treatment room to see Claire – but they never made it. As they approached the door they heard a nurse shouting: 'Come quick'.

The Pecks, overcome with fear, returned to the TV room. Again they asked the Sister if Claire was going to die. 'I hope not,' she replied. 'Were things getting worse?' asked Sue. 'Yes,' admitted the Sister, 'they are, but the staff are doing everything they can.'

With Claire at crisis point David asked if they could see their daughter because, if she was going to die, they wanted to be with her. As Sue and David walked into the treatment room they were stunned by what they found. David closes his eyes as he recalls the scene. 'The crash team was still working on Claire, they were giving her heart massage, electric shock and injections into her heart. She was surrounded by people, Beverley Allitt amongst them. They were all sweating, busy, working flat out as though they had been trying for a long time to save her.

'When they saw us they all stood back to let us look. I remember Sue saying: "Stop it. I think she's had enough." I wanted them to leave her as well.'

David recalls: 'Allitt was sitting right behind us, all she did was stare at us, she just watched and listened.'

Sue broke down and cried as she remembered the sight. 'Claire was dead, it was obvious, but they hadn't given up hope. I suppose there was a one in a thousand chance they might pull her back, and they still wanted to carry on.'

David still lives with the memory. 'We gave Claire a kiss. She was laid on a white table with a light shining on her. She had a lot of holes in her chest where they had injected her. She was very pale, almost white. They said they would carry on, and they asked us to go back to the TV room, but we realised we had lost her. Until then we hadn't really thought she would go . . .'

In the next cubicle Sue Phillips was sitting at baby Katie's bedside when Nurse Allitt walked in to tell her that Claire was dead.

Sue Phillips said: 'She just walked in and started to talk. She just wanted to tell me every detail of what had happened. My Becky was dead, and there I was with Katie, and I couldn't stop her talking. She said the worst bit was when Sue Peck wanted to hold on to Claire in her arms, and wouldn't let go. She wouldn't believe she was dead.

'She was asking Dr Porter to prove that Claire wasn't alive any more. Bev said Claire still had all the monitors on, and Dr Porter had to turn each one off so she could see it was running in a straight line and there was no sign of life.

'He showed her the straight line where the heartbeat should have been and only then did Sue Peck finally agree to let Claire go. Bev was in tears and she told me she had to tell someone. She just had to speak to somebody about what had happened. It was an awful time because Becky had only been dead for seventeen days.

'But Bev was so upset. There were tears rolling down her face.' The truth was very different. Sue Peck had not asked Dr Porter to prove Claire was dead. Neither had the doctor pointed to the straight line on the monitor to prove there was no sign of life. But at the time, Sue Phillips had no reason to doubt the nurse she trusted as a friend.

Nurse Allitt should have gone off duty, but she told Sue Phillips that her pal and housemate Tracy Jobson was working and she could not face going home to an empty house.

While Allitt was in tears in the cubicle with Sue Phillips, Claire's heartbroken parents collapsed, sobbing, in the TV lounge nearby. It was around 8.15pm. Ten minutes later Dr Porter, soaking wet with perspiration from the effort of trying to save Claire, appeared and told them he was terribly sorry but their little girl was dead. There was nothing more he could do.

The couple walked back to the treatment room to be with Claire. Asthma had killed their little girl, or so they thought. Yet when they met Dr Porter he seemed utterly bewildered by the tragedy.

Sue Peck remembers: 'He was just sitting there with his head in his hands, and he said: "This should never have happened." ' He told the Pecks that Claire's death was a million to one chance, a freak occurrence he could not explain. 'He told us that children die from asthma when they are untreated. In his opinion the chances were a million to one that a child could die while actually being treated in hospital. He was very distraught.'

It was Sue Peck's parents who began to ask questions about Claire's death. Why had the doctor said Claire shouldn't have died? What had he meant by that? They didn't understand. Sue and David were confused, too, but the specialist had told them it had been a million to one chance. 'We simply thought we had been very unlucky,' said Sue.

Still reeling from the shock of it all the Pecks were asked to stay at the hospital to meet the coroner's officer.

The hospital chaplain, the Rev. Shelton, who had conducted Liam Taylor's funeral service at the crematorium and buried Becky Phillips in his churchyard at Manthorpe, arrived and tried to comfort them.

Sue's father and brother went to the chapel of rest and identified Claire's body to the police. It was 11pm before Sue's father was able to drive the couple back home.

As he was leaving the hospital Sue's father overheard two nurses talking about the tragedy. He was within earshot when one nurse said: 'Not another one . . .' It was a throwaway comment that made no sense at the time. Sue and David had no idea that three other children had already died.

The next day Sue's father, Eric, returned to Grantham to collect a copy of the death certificate from the coroner's office. Once more an odd comment made him wonder about Claire's death. As he waited for the certificate a woman at reception remarked: 'Crikey, not another one. There's been a lot at Grantham hospital recently . . .'

A post mortem was held on Wednesday, 24 April, when the pathologist reported that asthma was the cause of Claire's death, which David and Sue accepted. For the fourth time the pathologist had decided that death was due to 'natural causes'. There would be no need, once again, for an inquest to be held.

Dr Porter, however, had taken a blood sample as Claire clung to life by a thread. It was a sample that was later analysed as doubt increased about the real cause of the children's deaths.

Sue said: 'We only found out about the blood sample a long time later. If he hadn't done that then they would never have known the answers. I am sure that Dr Porter suspected there was something wrong.'

Claire's funeral took place on 26 April. David and Sue still found it hard to believe that Claire was dead. All the time they kept remembering what the doctor had said about Claire's death being a chance in a million.

Claire's death had a profound effect on Sue and Peter Phillips. They had no way of knowing that Timothy Hardwick had died, but they did know that Liam Taylor, Becky and now Claire had all lost their lives on Ward Four – and they were determined to ask questions. They demanded a meeting with the hospital's general manager, Martin Gibson, wanting to know why the ward was still open, still taking in more sick children, despite all that had happened. They had heard suggestions that there was a virus on the ward causing children to have heart attacks. Peter recalls: 'It was a few days after Claire had died and we heard people talking on the ward about this virus, saying it was causing the kids to have heart attacks, and we had even heard some of the staff mention the rumour. If that was the case we wanted to know why they'd not shut the ward straight away.

'I told Martin Gibson: "There are kids dying on that ward . . ." But he said they couldn't close the place unless there was concrete evidence of something like Legionnaires Disease or meningitis, and they'd swabbed the walls, done all the checks and found absolutely nothing.'

Sue and Peter lost their tempers. It was the first time they had come face to face with Mr Gibson and they were in no mood for his assurances that the ward was free from disease. Sue remembers: 'We went at him like a bull in a china shop. He was trying to be nice, like a caring, considerate person, but we weren't in the mood. He said he could understand why I was mad, he'd have been mad if his daughter had died. He was trying to pacify us and he said he'd not heard talk of any heart virus. We were no happier when we left his office.'

The job of carrying out the first investigation into the deaths of babies on the Children's Ward at the Grantham and Kesteven Hospital fell on the shoulders of a former policeman. Tall, grey-haired Maurice Stonebridge-Foster was the coroner's officer, always the first person to be informed of any 'sudden death'.

He had been coroner's officer for six years after he retired from the Lincolnshire police force. He was a 'bobby' through and through. He'd never wanted the exalted heights and had never progressed from the ranks of police constable, spending most of his twenty-six years in the force in uniform, pounding the beat as a 'village copper', or at police stations in the bigger towns of Boston and Grantham, before landing the job assisting the coroner.

His three children were grown up; a son and one daughter were in the navy and another daughter was training to be a radiographer. His hobby was breeding King Charles spaniels; these had won him numerous prizes at dog shows all over the country, including Crufts, and he proudly carried a picture of his dogs in his wallet.

But, as coroner's officer in Grantham, dead bodies were his life and as much a routine to him as speeding drivers were to the traffic cops.

And when he 'put in his ticket' to leave the force, in October 1990, he continued life with the dead, staying in his old job as a civilian coroner's officer, working from the same office, with the same daily routine, investigating all of the 400-plus sudden deaths in and around Grantham each year.

His job, on behalf of the coroner, Mr John Pert, was to examine any sudden death – road-crash victims, suicides, falls, factory accidents, air crashes, electrocutions – the list was endless – and inform the coroner of his findings. He found himself most days in the mortuary at the Grantham and Kesteven Hospital where he would witness the clinical, sometimes grisly, job of post mortem examinations carried out by the pathologist and his mortuary staff. If the medical experts decided that death was from natural causes and there was nothing suspicious, then there would be no need for the coroner to hold an inquest.

If there was any death that was not natural, the coroner would hold a public inquest to establish the basic three points – when, where and how the unfortunate victim died.

Maurice Stonebridge-Foster, like coroner's officers all over the country, would prepare the evidence for the coming inquest, organise the witnesses and medical experts, and comfort relatives in their grief. It was not everyone's idea of a great job, but the former policeman liked it as much as any job he'd done in the force. 'It's the most useful job I have ever done,' was his view.

At the age of fifty he had never been a detective but, in April 1991, six months after he had 'retired' as a policeman, Stonebridge-Foster found himself the first to be called to Ward Four at the Grantham and Kesteven Hospital – never once suspecting that he was in the front line of what was to be the biggest murder investigation ever carried out at a hospital in Britain.

One 'sudden death' after another from the Children's Ward piled on to his desk but nothing he heard raised his suspicions. The regular pathologist was off sick so the routine post mortems were carried out by stand-in pathologists Dr Klaus Chen and Dr Terry Marshall. In all cases, they stated that, in their opinion, each of the children had died from natural causes.

No inquest, the coroner decided, was needed.

Mr Stonebridge-Foster later defended the decision. He said: 'I don't think I missed anything. As far as I was concerned they were just sudden deaths of sick children in hospital. There was nothing suspicious. Other children died naturally in the hospital at the same time, and there was nothing suspicious about their deaths either. There was nothing abnormal.

'It wasn't a case of a baby having a knife in its back or being covered in bruises. They were in hospital because they were sick and, unfortunately, sick children die. Some of the parents said they couldn't understand what was happening. They said they thought something was wrong. But that is a normal reaction from a parent at a time when they are so upset at losing their child.

'The worst cases for me were those parents who had lost their baby. But we look at between 400 and 500 deaths a year and there's usually about eighty inquests.

'I realised the deaths all came within a short period at the hospital but sometimes it happens like that; there may be a run of deaths in one place. But when the cause of the deaths was natural causes, I accepted it. There were no unnatural deaths, so there was no need for the coroner to hold inquests.'

Much later, after the new evidence on the causes of death emerged, inquests into all four cases were held.

Coroner Mr Pert sat in front of the parents of Liam Taylor, Timothy Hardwick, Becky Phillips and Claire Peck at Grantham Guildhall and said: 'In forty years, I have never had such tragic circumstances brought before me.'

7. Secret Cameras

When twelve policemen move in to begin a major investigation at a hospital one might suppose that everyone from the cleaner to the kitchen cat would know about it; that there would be the clump of size 11 shoes in the corridors, and white cars with red stripes and blue lights in the car park announcing: 'The police are here.'

But when the team of detectives moved in to the Grantham and Kesteven General Hospital on 1 May 1991 they were so discreet that their arrival passed almost without notice. Most people in the hospital had no idea for several weeks that there was any police investigation under way and even when, much later, some nurses and hospital staff did begin to realise it, many of them thought it was because one of the nurses had had some money stolen – such was the lack of awareness of criminal activities on Ward Four.

Detective Superintendent Stuart Clifton, the man leading the police enquiry team, is quietly spoken with an easy smile and a reputation for tenacity. He is also a 'thinking' policeman who found time to gain a BA in social sciences from the Open University.

Married with two sons, he had joined the police out of boredom in February 1966 after first qualifying as a quantity surveyor in the construction industry. His training had given him an eye for detail that was to become invaluable in his new job.

He was stationed at Boston, then transferred all over Lincolnshire. Promotions took him right to the top as operational head of Lincolnshire CID.

At the hospital Supt Clifton and his team first sought the opinions of the two chief paediatricians, Dr Nelson Porter and Dr Charith Sena Nanayakkara. He met them hoping for answers, perhaps even clues, but he went away with more questions than answers from the two doctors who didn't agree with each other.

Dr Porter told Supt Clifton that something untoward was going on and Dr Nanayakkara was not so sure. The detectives hadn't expected such a conflict of opinion, right at the beginning of the enquiry, between the two experts on whom they had hoped to rely. As he listened to the technical medical jargon, Stuart Clifton had instant misgivings about his new task and was overheard to remark in a whisper: 'I wish I was on leave!'

One detective said: 'Dr Porter just had this feeling that something had been going on but he didn't know what.'

He added: 'The hospital authorities had already done checks, swabbed the ward, wondering whether it was Legionnaires Disease. They hadn't thought there was anything criminal happening, that's not what they were looking for.

'But Dr Porter seemed to have already made up his mind that he didn't like the look of what had been happening on his ward. He had been to a British Paediatric Association conference where they had talked about children being tampered with in hospital, usually by their parents. Something must have clicked because after he got back to Grantham he phoned the hospital manager, Mr Gibson, at home. He was so worried about the number of children collapsing on his ward that he wanted to suggest to Mr Gibson that the hospital install video surveillance cameras to monitor what was happening in each and every cubicle.'

Similar 'spy on the ward' cameras had been hidden at a London hospital where a child had been suffering from unexplained fits. The secret cameras later filmed the mother deliberately putting a pillow over her child's face, until the youngster went into a fit. Then the mother could be seen building herself up into a frenzy before screaming for help.

Dr Porter had made the call to Mr Gibson on the Friday evening, three days before Claire Peck was to die on Ward Four. But Mr Gibson was not at home and he could only leave a message. Still worried, Dr Porter drew up his own action-list during the weekend, cataloguing what he would do 'when we had the next one'. But on Monday teatime Claire had collapsed before any of his suggestions could be initiated.

When the police arrived, Dr Porter asked again

for Ward Four to be put under surveillance. Detectives installed one of the closed-circuit video spy cameras over the main entrance to the ward in a position where they could monitor round-the-clock who might be slipping in unnoticed on to Ward Four.

The complexity of the medical evidence now convinced Supt Clifton that he needed a medical adviser to consult and interpret the opinions he was being given. He called in David Hull, a distinguished consultant paediatrician from Nottingham who had been chairman at the conference which had been attended by Dr Porter a few days earlier. Supt Clifton asked him to begin by carrying out a new medical review of nineteen cases, including all children who had died at the hospital or within forty-eight hours of leaving.

By now he had set up an incident room at Grantham Police Station, manned by a detective sergeant and eleven other officers, and set about looking for evidence. The enquiry was to be the most difficult case any of the officers had ever encountered. It was different because they would normally have started with a murder weapon – knife or a bullet in the back of the victim – and there would be a motive – love, jealousy, greed or whatever.

But here, all the post mortems had already been done and all the children had been found by pathologists to have died from natural causes.

Supt Clifton had to turn the clock back and reinvestigate everything that had been done before. It took him into a new world of medical science where policemen were not expected to be particularly knowledgeable. Hoping for assistance from parents who were already emotionally torn apart by what had happened to their children, he called in the force's Family Support Unit, a group of experienced policemen and women normally used in delicate child-abuse cases.

They spent ten days interviewing parents of the children who had died or been lucky to survive, asking them if they suspected anything. The results were disappointing. In the main, parents believed their children had been extremely well looked after on Ward Four; many were full of praise for the nurses and doctors who had worked so hard to save their children. They didn't welcome police officers asking them to recall upsetting times, no matter how delicately they probed.

For three weeks the police scoured the hospital records, checked the case histories of every child who had passed through the ward and analysed every single emergency in the hospital's 'bad run'.

Discussions sometimes went on into the night during 'debriefing' sessions at the Blue Pig, the squad's adopted pub - a sixteenth-century inn which served Whitbread bitter and an array of four real ales, Castle Eden, Flowers, Boddingtons and Websters.

There had been twenty-four separate incidents in the space of sixty days when children had suffered cardiac arrests, respiratory failures and heart attacks. The casualty 'crash team' hadn't been summoned every time but, even so, the sheer volume was astonishing when, normally, the detectives were told, the crash team might expect one call-out to the children's ward in a year, twice at the most.

How could that be simply a 'bad run'? The way the police saw it, this must be more than bad luck.

But suspicion was not enough and evidence was nowhere to be found.

Mr Hull produced his initial report into the nineteen cases he had examined and his conclusions were also far from encouraging. He reported that, in his view, there were no more than three incidents worthy of further investigation, and two of those might be questionable.

After three weeks they had got nowhere and every avenue had turned into a cul-de-sac. There was so little progress that they almost gave in and walked away from Ward Four, empty-handed.

There was a feeling that the case was going nowhere. Where, after all, was the evidence?

Only the persistence of Supt Clifton kept the investigation going. He was convinced that something just didn't add up. It was the sort of instinctive feeling that detectives cannot always explain. A colleague remarked later: 'He just wouldn't let go. He just kept saying he knew something wasn't right. He had a gut feeling about it.'

Supt Clifton decided to plough everything into his one and only lead – the blood tests on five-month-old Paul Crampton whose sugar level had plunged so low he had nearly died three times.

Paul had been transferred to the Queen's Medical Centre in Nottingham where his blood had been tested. It revealed a higher than normal level of insulin, a reading of 148 milli-units per litre of blood, the calibration used to measure minute quantities. That was far, far higher than it should have been. A normal level would be between 4 and 6.

The hospital ordered a second check which showed that, by then, the level in Paul's blood had dropped to 90. But a sample had also been taken earlier as a matter of routine at the Grantham and Kesteven General Hospital; this had been despatched to a specialist laboratory at Cardiff University for detailed analysis.

The results were totally unexpected.

Cardiff reported an insulin level 'in excess of 500'. What was even more worrying was that the laboratory couldn't tell Supt Clifton exactly how much higher than 500 - their equipment couldn't measure levels beyond that.

Supt Clifton thought at first that this was the proof that Paul had been given a massive dose of insulin, enough to kill him.

But he was to find it wasn't as simple as that.

Doctors explained that, in young children, the body sometimes produced insulin naturally in erratic and often high amounts. Big readings often indicated a tumour in the pancreas, secreting insulin into the body. Supt Clifton was told the level could sometimes soar as high as 1,000.

But was Paul suffering from such a tumour?

More tests revealed that he wasn't, so what had caused such an enormous reading?

Another factor added to the mystery and fuelled Supt Clifton's growing anxiety. When the body manufactures its own insulin, it also produces another substance called C-Peptide at exactly the same rate. If Paul's sky-high insulin level had been produced naturally, tests would detect an equally high C-Peptide reading. But, in Paul's blood, the C-Peptide was almost normal.

Supt Clifton decided to consult Britain's leading expert on insulin to ask for an explanation. He telephoned Vincent Marks, professor of bio-chemistry at the University of Surrey, vice-president of the Royal College of Pathologists and formerly president of the Association of Clinical Bio-Chemists. Professor Marks was just about to set off from Guildford for an art exhibition in the seaside resort of Scarborough with his wife, an accomplished artist and sculptor. He agreed, however, to make a detour to Grantham and the two men arranged to meet at the Angel and Royal where they talked about the findings over a pint of best Bass bitter.

Supt Clifton outlined the case to him, explaining how children had been falling ill and dying at his local hospital. The professor listened to the unfolding story and digested the figures so far available.

By the end of the discussion Professor Marks was convinced that something untoward had been happening. He was as sure as he could be that, yes, insulin had been administered to little Paul

Crampton. There was no other possible explanation for the reading in excess of 500.

The professor offered the help of another expert at the university, Dr David Teal, who would do more tests on the Crampton blood sample, only half of which had been used at Cardiff. The remaining half of Paul's blood was moved from Cardiff to the laboratory at Guildford which was equipped accurately to measure higher levels.

When the Guildford result came back, it was staggering.

The test showed an insulin level of an incredible *forty-three thousand* milli-units per litre of blood, a figure virtually unknown in the medical world. The only comparable reading had been found in a doctor who had deliberately injected himself with a huge overdose to commit suicide.

It was equivalent, in a baby, to having an entire 10ml syringe full of insulin pumped into the body in one dose. Even if Paul had a tumour – and the police knew he hadn't – a level as high as 43,000 could not be explained.

Now, at last, here was the proof that the child had been overdosed on a huge scale; detectives realised just how lucky Paul had been to survive.

Insulin, first discovered in 1922 by two Canadian professors, is not a drug but a protein naturally produced by the pancreas.

Too little insulin in the blood produces the classic symptoms of diabetes – a chronic thirst, feelings of lethargy and tiredness and loss of weight. Too much brings on trembling, shaking, sweating, fits and causes the victim painlessly to collapse, ultimately into a coma, which, if not treated with a supply of sugar, will be fatal.

Insulin at the Grantham and Kesteven General Hospital was kept, the detectives discovered, in much the same way as in hospitals all over the country. It was not a dangerous drug, to be stored with the morphine, but was kept on the ward in a locked fridge, ready for use. No accurate records were ever considered necessary because, as in most hospitals, nurses had a habit of drawing more than they required into the syringe and squirting the remainder away. It was kept and used in much the same way, and with the same security, as other everyday essential medicines.

But Supt Clifton now wanted to know whether Paul had been given an injection of insulin deliberately or could it have been an awful mistake? Suspicions grew when he discovered that the key to the fridge had gone missing. Nurse Allitt said that she had gone to open it but found that the key had vanished from the key ring. A thorough search was made but the key was never traced.

Ward manager Moira Onions had been asked by doctors to carry out an urgent review of the drug supplies to the ward. They wanted to know whether there could have been a mix-up in the labelling. Could Paul have innocently been given the wrong drug by mistake? Could there have been another child on the ward who should have been receiving insulin instead?

Supt Clifton, however, still felt that the overdose had been no accident and, if it wasn't, then he had to know who could do such a thing. It had to be someone who had easy access, someone who was trusted enough to get close to the child, administer an overdose and not be noticed. The 'spy' camera was producing nothing and there had not been another single incident on Ward Four since the day the police were called in.

Detectives began questioning every nurse whose duties had taken them to the ward, asking them in minute detail what they remembered of the emergencies, where they had been and who had been with them at the time children had died or collapsed.

Still, for many of them, the reason for the police investigation was a mystery. A detective said: 'In the end we had to call all the nurses together to a meeting and tell them exactly what we were doing and that we needed their cooperation.

'They had all taken an oath, not to talk about patients, and as a result the word just didn't get round for weeks on end.'

Some of the nurses suffered feelings of guilt and blamed themselves for not realising what had happened. Others were convinced they were under suspicion. Nurse Kathy Lock, who worked on the Children's Ward, said: 'I was there most of the time during the period that the police were investigating and yet it had never occurred to me in any way whatsoever that it could be deliberate. It was the last thing we had thought about.

'It's not the sort of thing you could ever imagine happening in a hospital.'

Another nurse said: 'We realised that we were all suspects and some of us were interviewed half a dozen times. We had looked after the children at various times so I suppose at that stage we were all looking at one another, and wondering . . .'

Supt Clifton and his team drew a chart, detailing each one of the emergencies, and pinned it to the wall. They were looking for a common thread – a pattern which would make sense of the events.

Armed with the detailed staff-rota lists, they drew rough graphs on the wall of the incident room. Supt Clifton wanted to know if there were any nurses who had been regularly on duty when the incidents happened.

As he ticked off each event, one name recurred time . . . and time . . . and time again.

It appeared alongside every one of the twenty-four incidents that had occurred on Ward Four during the sixty days.

The name was that of Nurse Beverley Allitt.

The newly qualified SEN, still only twenty-two, was taken under arrest at breakfast-time on the morning of Monday, 3 June – five weeks after the start of the investigation – to the grey stone Grantham police headquarters. She was questioned for two days about Paul Crampton, sleeping the night in a 10 × 11 foot cell.

She spent both days protesting her innocence, never once admitting any responsibility, totally denying she was in any way to blame. In some instances she insisted she had not even been present when particular children had suffered unexplained relapses on her ward; it was always someone else.

Her calmness under questioning surprised Supt Clifton and his team. It was the first time in her life that the quietly spoken village girl had ever been locked up by police and they were astonished that she could remain so cool, with no sign of tears or nerves. One policeman said: 'You would have thought she was on a Sunday School outing. There was no reaction from her. It was more a case of her saying, "Can I have something to read?"

'You would have thought she had booked into the Ritz for a holiday.'

He added: 'Being kept in a police cell is a very demeaning experience but she seemed to just take it in her stride.'

Nurse Beverley Gail Allitt was released on police bail the following evening and sent home on extended leave by the hospital at the suggestion of the police.

8. Beverley – the Godmother

The joy of having surviving twin Katie back from the dead sent a welcome surge of hope into the lives of Sue and Peter Phillips. Determined to look now to a brighter future, and totally unaware of the police investigation at the hospital, they asked Nurse Beverley Allitt if she would agree to be Katie's godmother.

Peter explained: 'We were so pleased and happy with what she'd done. We'd seen how her quick thinking probably saved Katie. We had seen her rushing from the room at the hospital, holding Katie in her arms, shouting for the 'crash team', when she discovered she had stopped breathing. We thought that, if she hadn't have been there, Katie would have died. What she'd done was wonderful. Why shouldn't the girl, who saved her life, become her godmother?'

Sue said: 'We asked Bev at the hospital, on Katie's first day back from Nottingham, if she would consider becoming her godmother. She said, "Yes," without a second thought. She seemed to be over-joyed at the prospect.'

Allitt was so pleased that she went shopping for her little goddaughter and bought her a charming baby-gro.

Sue said: 'Katie came home from hospital for the day on Friday, 10 May. I remember it because it was a glorious, sunny spring day which was so warm we were able to sit out in the garden.

'I also remember it because it was the first time that Bev came to our house. We hadn't expected her, but she arrived about 3pm, still dressed in her blue check nurses' uniform because she had just come off duty.

'We were all sitting out in the garden and Peter had even put up the big sun umbrella. Katie was in her buggy under the umbrella and Bev brought the present for her. Bev was fine. She was happy, smiling and we were pleased to see her. She was, after all, going to be Katie's godmother. My mum and dad were here too and, like us, they were delighted she'd made the effort to come.'

Someone made her a cup of tea and, later, she sipped a cold drink with them as she stayed for the remainder of the sunny afternoon.

Sue recalls: 'We were still a bit nervous about Katie's condition and it felt comforting to have a nurse with us. I was constantly going up to the buggy just to make sure she was all right. She still had the Apnia Alarm fitted to her chest, that was with her all the time, but it still felt right to check.

'I remember talking to Bev about it and she was very reassuring. She said she was sure we had nothing to worry about. Katie was going to be fine.'

Sue still couldn't manage to cope with Katie being at home permanently, so the hospital allowed her to take her baby back at night to sleep in Ward Four where she continued her stay as a part-time patient, going home whenever Sue and Peter could cope.

The following Wednesday, Sue and Peter decided they were ready to have Katie at home permanently and she was finally discharged from hospital. Sue said: 'I felt very confident that day and I knew that the longer we left her at the hospital, the more difficult it would become to take her home.'

She said: 'We brought Katie home dressed in the pink-and-white baby-gro Bev had bought for her. It was such a lovely, sunny and warm day again that we decided to walk from the hospital, pushing Katie in her buggy. It's only a five-minute walk and it was wonderful.'

It was a relief having Katie home for good, although Sue couldn't bear the thought of going into the nursery where the twins had slept those first few hours on the night Becky died. Peter swapped the rooms round so that Becky's cot was gone and Katie slept in the front bedroom. At least it looked and felt different and there were no awful memories to haunt them.

The next day Allitt, now a growing family friend and a shoulder for Sue to lean on, arrived at the house around lunchtime. Smiling, she picked up Katie to give her a cuddle and Sue was delighted when she offered to feed her. Sue left her sitting on the settee in the lounge with Katie on her lap feeding her with her bottle.

What a good friend she was turning out to be. Allitt was off duty and ended up staying for four or five hours. The two women were soon going on shopping trips together, pushing Katie around Grantham in her buggy.

Sue said: 'She knew I was still a bit apprehensive about having Katie at home. It was just so reassuring having Bev around. She said to me: "You are bound to feel like that, Sue. Don't worry about it."'

The next day Katie was snuffling with a cold and wasn't interested in feeding and, taking no chances, the emergency doctor decided she should go back into hospital, just for observation. Katie was admitted to Ward Four where she was placed in a cot in Cubicle Two. She was congested and doctors prescribed simple nose drops and anti-biotics to clear up what seemed like a dose of flu.

Sue stayed with her and, by the Monday, after two nights in the hospital, Katie was much better. When doctors insisted, however, that she must stay in for about a week, Sue was reassured that Allitt was on duty and assigned to look after her little goddaughter-to-be. Katie recovered so quickly that, by Wednesday, 29 May, paediatrician Dr Nanayakkara told them they could take her home.

It was a week later before the Phillips saw Beverley Allitt again. Unknown to Sue and Peter, the police investigations had been in full swing on Ward Four for more than a month. Allitt made no mention of the police enquiries, her arrest and suspension from duty, when she popped in for half an hour for a cup of coffee. She blamed her absence on the fact that she had been working hard.

She returned the following Tuesday, the day Peter kept a long-awaited date with surgeons to have a vasectomy – a decision they had taken even before Becky had died. She wanted to ask if she could take Katie out on a trip to visit a friend.

Sue's mother, who was in the house babysitting, asked her to wait until Sue got home from hospital; Allitt was still at the house when Sue returned. She asked if she could take James as well as Katie to the park. Sue saw nothing wrong with the request.

'I wasn't worried at all when they went off,' she said. 'But they were gone for ages and that's when I became anxious. After about two hours I was beginning to panic a bit, wondering if something had gone wrong. I rang Bev's house, about a mile away, but there was no reply. I just sat there and waited.'

Sue wasn't to know that Allitt was doing what she'd always done when looking after children; she had taken them to show her grandmother in the rural village of Corby Glen, eight miles south-east of Grantham, where she had lived until she started work at the hospital. She finally returned with Katie and James, four and a half hours later, by which time Sue was frantic.

'She could see how upset I had been but she told me she hadn't meant to worry me. She said: "I just thought you could do with the break." '

The following day, Wednesday, 12 June, Beverley Allitt called in again, arriving at about

4pm. This time she wanted to take James out for another trip.

She said she was going to pick up her friend, Tracy Jobson, who also worked as a nurse at the hospital, and they were driving to Peterborough to visit Tracy's mother. They were planning to stop at a McDonald's on the way. She turned to three-year-old James and told him: 'It's OK, James, you can come with me.'

The little boy was delighted and rushed to put on his shoes and get himself ready even before Sue had said he could go.

Allitt casually told her for the first time about the police investigation that was under way on the Children's Ward at the hospital. It should have hit Sue like a bombshell. But Allitt announced it so calmly that to begin with, Sue didn't imagine for a minute that it was important.

'All she told me was that some people were being questioned at the hospital. She didn't seem worried about it and she certainly wasn't nervous. She said the police had been interviewing staff. Then she told me: "I don't know what they are getting at but they are asking a lot of questions about Paul Crampton." '

Sue knew about Paul Crampton who had nearly died after collapsing on Ward Four. She remembered how his mother, Kath, had been in tears because he had been producing too much insulin in his body.

But even now, with Allitt breaking news of a police investigation, Sue didn't suspect anything untoward. 'I just thought it was some sort of routine investigation into what had happened. She told me it was all about Paul Crampton. It was at the time when all three of ours were in the hospital – Becky, Katie and James. I knew Paul had been very seriously ill and people had been full of praise for how Bev had helped save him.'

As she stood listening to her friend, Sue was baffled but not unduly worried. It flashed through her mind that perhaps the authorities thought someone had got into the hospital and tampered with Paul.

She could see no reason to stop James going off with Allitt and he was already excited about his impending trip out.

So, at about 4pm, the bubbly, fair-haired chatterbox they always called 'Jampot' walked through the front door, hand in hand with Allitt. Sue watched as they drove off in Bev's white Ford Fiesta with James strapped in his seat belt at the front alongside her. This time Katie stayed at home.

What Sue didn't know was that Allitt was already effectively suspended from duty at the hospital after being sent home on 'extended leave'. She had made no mention of her two days at the police station where she'd spent the night locked in a cell. She hadn't said that she'd been singled out by the police as the prime suspect.

Sue went back to her ironing and wondered what it was all about.

At 7.30pm Allitt brought James home. Safe and

sound. They had had a 'great day', she said. She had picked up Tracy from the hospital and driven them both to Peterborough, to the home of Tracy's mother, Eileen, at Orton Goldhay, just off the A1. It was only a forty-minute drive but they had also kept their promise to the youngster by dropping in at McDonald's en route.

But Allitt looked unusually anxious and worried about something. She asked to have a word with Sue, just the two of them, woman to woman. (Tracy and her mother were outside, waiting in the car.) Sue led the nurse into the kitchen where Sue recalls how Allitt announced: 'There's something I want to tell you.'

Sue wasn't ready for what she had to say but remembers how Allitt, speaking calmly, started from the beginning, saying: 'Last Monday morning I was woken up at 7.30 by a hammering on my front door.

'I want you to hear this from me, Sue, before anyone else gives you any gossip. When I got up, there were all these CID officers and a police-woman there and they said they wanted to talk to me. I asked them if they could wait while I got dressed and they didn't mind, but they wanted to talk to me down at the police station. I went down with them and they asked me a lot of questions and tape-recorded the interview.'

Sue was dumbstruck.

She had noticed that, all that week, Allitt was not at the hospital but she had assumed she was either on leave or off sick.

Allitt went on: 'They've accused me of trying to murder Paul Crampton.'

Sue listened in amazement as Allitt told her the police had kept her in the cells until Tuesday afternoon.

Sue said: 'She looked me straight in the eye and said: "Can you believe it? Me? After all the kids I have tried to save."'

As the the two women talked Sue poured out words of comfort to her frightened friend. Yes, how could they doubt her? she said. After all, she'd seen her save her own daughter Katie with her own eyes.

Allitt went on: 'They think it's me because I was nursing him. It's because I was there. The police asked me straight outright if I had tried to murder Paul Crampton with insulin. I told them I had not. All they kept on about was Paul Crampton.'

Allitt told Sue that she had been allowed a solicitor. She had repeated so many times that she was innocent that, finally, she had lost her temper with one policeman and told him bluntly: 'I'm not making something up just to please you.'

Outside, Tracy and her mother still sat waiting in the car, and Allitt declined Sue's offer to invite them inside.

Tracy had been pulled in, too, for questioning by the police team, she said. The detectives had asked Tracy if she had seen Allitt doing anything suspicious with a syringe or drugs.

When she finally got home on Tuesday, the police had gone right through her home, searching for any possible evidence. Her white Fiesta had been virtually 'pulled to bits', stripped down by the searching detectives.

Sue listened in disbelief. Allitt threw Sue one challenging question. She pleaded: 'Sue, how can I prove I didn't do anything to that boy?'

Sue made an instant decision to do everything she could to help her. She said: 'I felt so sorry for her, really ever so sorry. She said she had told them everything she knew but she was worried they were going to nail her for something she had not done.'

Allitt had first been interviewed at the hospital while she was on duty, along with other nurses, she explained. But then she broke more surprising news, telling Sue that she had been suspended from duty at the hospital and given police bail.

Sue remembers: 'She was very upset. She looked sad and drawn and worried, although there were no tears. I couldn't really take in what she was saying and, anyway, I was totally convinced that she was innocent. I didn't have a single doubt.

'The only child that the police had mentioned was Paul – there was nothing about Becky. And, anyway, I had no idea about how many children had died or how many had been taken ill at the hospital. I knew about some of the others but, in my mind, I had just put it down, at worst, as perhaps some kind of virus.'

Sue remembers asking: 'What could they charge you with?'

Allitt replied: 'Attempted murder.'

Sue gasped: 'Oh! Bloody hell!'

She was totally convinced that Allitt was innocent, a victim of some terrible mistake by the police. Sue wanted to help her prove it.

How could they try to pin something on Bev after all she had done to help so many children? How could they even think she could harm Paul Crampton?

Sue first offered Allitt the name of a solicitor whom she knew was good. Then she told her the names of two friends, David Thorpe and Ruth Lindsey, who were private detectives working in Grantham. Perhaps they could help. Allitt was delighted. Yes, she would see anyone who thought they could help her.

Peter, who had been sitting in the lounge while the two women talked in the kitchen, came in to be told briefly what had been said. He immediately added his words of comfort and support. 'Of course we'll help you,' he told Allitt. 'The whole idea that you could be involved is bloody ridiculous.'

Sue and Peter were so sure that the police were wrong that they even offered to pay the bill for the private investigators as a token of their gratitude for saving Katie's life.

The following day Peter, always the handyman, put back together the interior of Allitt's car after the attentions of the police as they searched it. He said: 'It was such a mess inside. They had taken the seat covers off and there were panels hanging off. It took hours to do it but I was happy just to be helping her.' They also kept their promise to arrange a meeting with the two private detectives.

Sue recalls Allitt finally leaving the house, with the words: 'Thank you for all you are doing for me. I am just glad someone is trying to help me.'

9. Beverley – the Angel

Beverley Allitt had wanted to be a nurse for as long as most people could remember. She didn't want to be just any nurse. Beverley had wanted, dreamed, longed, to be allowed to nurse children.

She was a chubby girl, plain but not unattractive, with short, cropped blonde hair. She had grown up surrounded by children in the village of Corby Glen, eight miles outside Grantham. Her love of children made her popular as a babysitter and villagers remember how she always liked playing with youngsters and taking them for walks.

The girl they knew had talked of nothing but becoming a nurse from about the age of twelve or thirteen. They had trusted her with children. They had seen her play with their children and take them for walks. They had seen her serving behind the counter of Pauline's village store to earn a few extra pounds when she was still a student at college.

They had seen her laugh, play pool and serve bar meals at the Fighting Cocks at the top of the road where she lived happily with her mother and father, younger brother Darren, and sisters Donna and Alison with whom she had shared a bedroom.

Neighbours were in no doubt that Beverley had been blessed with a normal, perfectly happy childhood. There was no hint in her background of lawlessness, rebellion or resentment. Beverley Allitt did not come from a broken home. She had not suffered the deprivation of being brought up in an inner-city slum.

The locals had seen her walking with her family to the village church of St John the Evangelist where they remembered her taking her confirmation vows when she was fourteen. They had seen her fall in love with village boy Steve Biggs, a strapping 6ft 2ins roadworker who was to become her fiancé.

Corby Glen lies in the valley of the River Glen, set in some of the finest sheep-farming country in Lincolnshire. Around 450 men, women and children live in this unspoiled corner of England. It's a place where everyone knows everyone else, and people stick together in times of trouble. There's the tiny junior school where Beverley had been a pupil until she was eleven, a post office, Pauline's store as well as a Co-op supermarket, a large village square which has stood unchanged for centuries, a church dating back to 1319 and three pubs, the Glaziers Arms, the Woodhouse Arms and the Fighting Cocks.

The council's travelling library van stops in the village square every Monday, and the mobile fish and chip shop parks there on a Tuesday night. On the hill above the village stands the comprehensive school where Beverley Allitt first spoke of being a nurse.

Jobs no longer abound on the local farms where only a handful of men can count on earning a living from the land. Beverley Allitt's father, Richard, worked for the Hay Wine Co. which has its warehouse round the corner from the village square. Otherwise, most of the villagers commute to and from local towns.

Locals still boast there's a community spirit in Corby Glen that's alive and kicking. That sense of belonging is evident every October when farmers gather from all over the country for the annual village sheep fair and auction. The whole village turns out to see the spectacle. There's a sheep-fair dance, a fun-fair for the children, military bands, clay-pigeon shooting, tug-o-war competitions, art and craft displays, pony rides and sheep by the thousand.

The village celebrated the 750th sheep fair on 10 October 1988 and, to mark the event, the entire population gathered in the village square to be photographed for posterity. It was a unique historical occasion and every single one of the villagers, all 446 of them, were there. Beverley Allitt stood beside her fiancé, Steve Biggs, to the right of the picture, with Steve sporting the moustache she had insisted he grew.

The framed photograph still hangs in the entrance of the Woodhouse Arms. A separate photograph was taken of forty-six people who had lived in the village for at least fifty years. Among them was Beverley's grandmother.

Beverley Allitt was a popular figure in Corby Glen

where her parents were respected by all; there had never been a hint of scandal in the family.

Her father's boss at the Hay Wine Co., Jeremy Marshall-Roberts, recalled: 'Beverley used to baby-sit for us when she was younger. She always had this affinity with children. She loved them, they liked her.'

Round the corner from the Allitts's tidy, red-brick semi, with its blue, glass-panelled front door, net curtains upstairs and down, and neat garden on three sides, lies Pauline's village store where Beverley had helped out at weekends when she was a teenager. Pauline recalled: 'Everyone always knew that Beverley wanted to go into nursing. She was always a popular girl. She'd worked here at the shop and knew a lot of people.'

Her grandmother, Dorothy Burrows, got used to the sight of Beverley arriving at her home in Bourne, Lincolnshire, with children, toddlers, and even babies, from the village of Corby Glen. On Sundays when Beverley's parents, Richard and Lillian, visited Grandma Burrows, Beverley would often take along a neighbour's child.

Dorothy had seen many of the children grow up. Some of them had even continued to visit with Richard and Lillian when, to her grandmother's delight, Beverley finally realised her ambition to start work at Grantham and Kesteven Hospital. There had been months of training, studies and exams to pass, duty on the geriatric ward, then, at last, the chance to fulfil her dreams and start on the Children's Ward.

Dorothy knew how much Beverley loved the job, treasured every moment, revelled in the contact with infants and their parents. It had been more than a job to Beverley, it had been a way of life.

Her grandmother sighed as she glanced at a photograph of Beverley, taken when she was a baby, which still hangs proudly on her front-room wall. 'You see, Beverley always had this way with children. She used to come with her mum and dad every Sunday afternoon without fail. She would bring children with her, they were neighbours' and friends' children from Corby Glen. Some were only babies, two or three months old. Sometimes she would bring two along, she'd take them for a walk, play with them, feed them at tea-time and even bath them sometimes. One little boy she used to get ready for bed before they went home. She always had this wonderful way with them.'

She went on: 'People in Corby Glen trusted Beverley with their children and some of the youngsters still go to Richard and Lillian's even now. If she'd got a bad name, then nobody would have let her have their kids. But they knew they could rely on her. I've heard people say she was the nicest girl in Corby Glen.'

Rachel Smith was Beverley's closest childhood friend. They grew up in the same street. Rachel lived with her mother and father at 16 Barleycroft, a smart terraced house just round the corner from the Fighting Cocks. Beverley lived across the cul-de-sac with her family at number 24. The two girls started on the same day at the village primary school.

Rachel noticed how Beverley took to mothering the local children even when she was only little herself. Rachel's first memory is of Beverley pushing her baby brother, Darren, in his pram when her friend was no older than six or seven. Rachel got used to seeing Beverley playing with younger children from around the village.

'She used to mother the little kids. You got used to seeing Beverley playing with the toddlers, pushing their prams or walking them up and down the road. We were in the same class at the primary school. Even then Beverley was on the chubby side, but she was always one of the brightest kids. She had plenty of ability so it was a bit of a surprise when she failed the test to go to the Girls' High School in Grantham. Mrs Thatcher was a pupil there once and, like me, I suppose Beverley was disappointed at missing out. She only failed by four points.'

The two girls found themselves drawn together from the day they started at Charles Read, the secondary-modern school on the hill above the village. 'I remember the night we went up to school with our parents. Beverley's mum and dad are smashing people. They put the girls from the primary school in one form, and the boys in another, so the two of us stayed together. From the beginning we got on fine.'

Rachel always knew that Beverley was going to be a nurse. When their class did a project on child

care, and was told to monitor the progress of a toddler week by week, Beverley was in her element.

'She used to love home economics and child
care was a part of that. I chose to spend time with
the people at the Fighting Cocks who'd got a little
baby. Bev picked the Warburtons who'd got a two-
year-old son. It involved going to see the kids a
couple of times every week, playing with them,
taking them out for walks, babysitting for them,
everything on a one-to-one basis. Bev was fourteen then; I think it was the first time I heard her
talk seriously about being a nurse. It wasn't a surprise. I mean, it was obvious then that it would suit
her although she never liked the sight of blood and
I used to tease her about that.'

Beverley joined the Girl Guides and, in the
summer, she would pack a picnic and walk for
miles through the fields and woods with fellow
guides Rachel and Dawn Greetham. Once the
three girls spent the whole day trekking from one
village to another, visiting seven neighbouring
parish churches in all.

There wasn't much night life for young girls in
Corby Glen but, once a month on a Friday night,
the village came alive with a disco in the village
hall near the church. The three pals would save up
their pocket money, spend 50p on a ticket, buy
cans of coke and a few bags of crisps, and let their
hair down dancing to Bananarama and Duran
Duran.

'We were fourteen or fifteen at the time and it
was the highlight of our social calendar,' recalls

Dawn. 'It would go on until midnight, but the three of us would normally leave around 11pm. We didn't have boyfriends, but we'd dance, and the boys would just stand around and watch. Eventually, after the vicar complained about the noise, they stopped having the discos altogether.'

Beverley and her friends weren't the kind to get into trouble. The nearest she, Rachel and Dawn ever got to breaking the law was pinching the odd apple when the orchards were full in mid summer. Dawn remembers clambering over garden walls and scaling apple trees in search of fresh fruit. 'We'd do a bit of scrumping, the three of us, borrowing the odd apple here and there. On mischievous nights we used to have a bit of fun tapping on windows in the village, then running off, but we were all just ordinary kids. We never misbehaved much. If we went out in the village we'd always be home on time.'

At school, Beverley hated sports lessons and managed to escape the cross-country runs and the hockey in the winter. Rachel said: 'She used to get out of it as much as she could. Bev was OK doing indoor sport but, if she had to do the cross-country running with the rest of us, she was always one of the last to finish. They had us going round the school field ten times, it was awful, and with Bev being a bit on the heavy side she hated it more than most of us.'

She became conscious of her weight. All her friends were slim and she was the biggest of the bunch, a good two stones too heavy, but she never bothered to cut down on her eating. She wore baggy clothes, jeans and jumpers away from school, and nobody ever saw her wearing a short skirt.

Rachel recalls how her friend lived a 'charmed life' at school. If she was messing about then it was always someone else the teacher caught. She would be the one with the idea for a prank or a bit of fun, but it was always someone else who did it.

Beverley never had a boyfriend while she was at school though she and Rachel did take on the job of scoring for the boys' basketball team.

'We used to have a laugh with the boys, but none of them would dare to tease Bev about her weight. I got the feeling they were actually a bit frightened of her. Most of the boys were smaller than her. Bev could always take care of herself. She wouldn't want to get into fights, she would always back off, but you got the impression she could handle herself.'

School headmaster John Gleeson remembers her dreams of wanting to become a nurse and her joy when she finally made it.

As he recalls: 'She was always on the chubby side, but a helpful, pleasant girl. It's a small school with around 240 pupils. We don't have the problems that exist in inner cities. We try to develop a warm atmosphere and, by and large, the children respond. Beverley was above average as a pupil and she did particularly well in home economics which dealt with child development and nursing, among other things. Nursing was always her chosen path and it really was no surprise when she left school and started a pre-nursing course at Grantham college.'

She had always been so pleasant, responsible and determined to realise her ambition. She left school in June 1985 with seven CSEs: French, English language, English literature, maths, biology, history and home economics. Her marks in home economics were so good she was awarded an O level pass.

Rachel became a regular visitor to her friend's home, which she remembers as a warm, loving environment, although Beverley would sometimes argue with her two sisters who shared her bedroom. The two friends would go babysitting together and Rachel noticed how Beverley was delighted when the baby woke up, seeing it as a bonus, a chance to cuddle and to play. 'When you're babysitting all you want is for the baby to stay asleep, but Bev loved them to wake up. It never bothered her, she had so much patience with kids, and she always got them back to sleep. She used to babysit for the Latters, the Warburtons and Sue Binner, who lived across from the Fighting Cocks. She wasn't that interested in making money out of it, it was more the opportunity to be with kids.'

In her spare time teenager Beverley worked at the village store or served bar meals at the pub to earn a few extra pounds. She had also become an accomplished pool player, capable of beating many of the lads at the Fighting Cocks; she could also play a mean game of darts.

Rachel had wanted to join the RAF to train as an air-traffic controller, but she failed the entrance exam. While she waited to re-sit the test she joined Beverley at Grantham college, travelling back and forth by bus each morning and night. It was there that Rachel met her future husband and when they married at Edenham parish church, just a few miles from Corby Glen, on 4 July 1987, Beverley made the day memorable by abandoning her baggy jumpers and jeans, and wearing a dress.

Eighteen-year-old Rachel moved to Scotland but returned frequently to Corby Glen. When baby son Garry was born Beverley fussed over him like an aunt. 'She always gave Garry a lot of attention when I went back to Corby Glen,' said Rachel. 'She would send me cardigans for him.' The girls lost touch but then, in September 1990, they met by chance when Rachel's sister gave birth at Grantham and Kesteven Hospital. The baby arrived prematurely and was in the special baby care unit. Beverley was there to see a fellow nurse who had given birth to twins. She was working on the Children's Ward by then and was delighted to see Rachel.

'I said she had done well getting the job she wanted. She asked where I was living and hadn't realised I had moved back to Grantham with my husband. We chatted, it was good to see her again.'

Beverley had to wait for her dream to come true. When her college course finished there had been no vacancies for student nurses at the Grantham and Kesteven Hospital; Beverley joined many of her friends on the dole. She hated being out of work, living on her Giro from the state, and she had to wait six months before she got the news that a job was finally hers. It was a moment to treasure and Beverley, by now eighteen, threw herself into her new life on the wards.

Her first decision was to leave Corby Glen and move into the nurses' home across the road from the hospital.

She trained as a student nurse for three years, studying whenever she got the chance. All that mattered was qualifying as a State Enrolled Nurse, and working with children.

Then, in mid-February 1991, she went for an interview at the Pilgrim Hospital in Boston, thirty miles from Grantham. She was in the process of finishing her training and had been working for the last six months on the Children's Ward at the Grantham and Kesteven Hospital. The Pilgrim Hospital was her big chance. But she was turned down for the job. She was told the reason she was being rejected was because she simply did not have enough experience treating very sick children.

The news was devastating. Allitt returned to Grantham wondering what the future held. The authorities at Grantham came to her rescue. They had been advertising for a staff nurse and hadn't received a single application, so they offered her a short-term contract for six months.

It was a stop gap, an opportunity to gain the experience she needed to reapply for the job at Boston.

She had six months to prove what she could do, to show she could cope.

10. Steve – Her One True Love

Allitt's decision to move from her home village of Corby Glen to near the hospital in Grantham came as a blow to boyfriend Steve Biggs, the first and only real love of her life.

She was dumpy, plain and overweight, never bothered to wear make-up, not the kind of girl to turn heads in Corby Glen. But Steve Biggs had been besotted from the night they'd first met in the bar of the Fighting Cocks in September 1987. She was drinking halves of lager with a girlfriend, dressed as always in jeans and a baggy sweat-shirt and, when he challenged her to a game of pool, she'd beaten him fair and square.

It was to be the first of many defeats for the shy, quietly spoken roadworker during a love affair in which he became totally dominated by Allitt's overwhelming strength of personality. Their battles and occasional sexual encounters were to last two and a half years – a strange, almost unreal relationship even when they got engaged and began to talk of marriage.

Steve remembers how Allitt would bully him,

sometimes attacking him with her fists, or even kneeing him in the groin, leaving him crying and rolling in agony on the floor. She grumbled about their love-making and twice, when they went away on holiday, she refused to share his bed, sleeping instead in a separate room with a girlfriend.

When she began openly to walk hand in hand in public with another girl, Steve began to worry that his girlfriend might be more interested in women than men. He became so concerned that, at one point, he finally plucked up the courage to ask Allitt: 'Are you a lesbian?' She totally denied it and insisted it had been 'just a joke'.

When he met Allitt she was still just seventeen, and he was eighteen, a new arrival in the village. He had been instantly swept off his feet.

Anxious to make new friends, and weary of sitting at home night after night in front of the TV, Steve had begun to visit the Fighting Cocks after work. When he spotted Allitt in the bar one of the regulars said she was a 'nice, quiet girl'. They played pool and began meeting at the pub.

At that time, Allitt had completed her pre-nursing course at Grantham college and was on the dole, waiting for an interview at the hospital. She was trying to fill her time babysitting and visiting friends in the village, but she was desperately bored and eager to start work.

'She hated not having much money but, for all that, she seemed happy and she used to laugh a lot. I thought she was a nice girl, very friendly and chirpy. She was good company.'

Steve found that romance with Allitt was a frustrating experience. She refused to let him walk her home right to her door, and always insisted he left her at the top of the road. Steve thought it was odd, but then the whole relationship would be peculiar.

Steve was very much the village boy. There had never been much excitement and drama in his life. His romantic encounters were limited to a brief and painful affair with a girl in the nearby town of Bourne where he had gone to secondary school. Steve was a beginner when it came to sex. Beverley Allitt, too, had no experience in the art of love. But, as they walked home one night from the Fighting Cocks, she concocted a fanciful tale that was designed to fill him with pity. At the time Steve had no idea that it was a lie aimed at winning his sympathy.

A year or so earlier Allitt had met one of Steve's former classmates from Bourne School. One of her pals had been going steady and persuaded her boyfriend to bring along Kevin Fowler for Beverley. Steve remembered the name from their days together at school. He had always disliked Fowler and recalled, as Allitt told the story, how they had once come to blows. He listened in astonishment as his girlfriend described her brief fling with Fowler.

They had been out together in a foursome a couple of times, enjoyed a few drinks at the pub but it hadn't been a serious relationship. They had just been friends – no more than that. But Allitt claimed it had ended in terrifying fashion with Fowler trying to rape her. She told Steve they were walking home when Kevin slipped behind a tree to spend a penny.

The next thing she knew he was holding her at knifepoint 'trying to get his way'. Allitt told the story in a matter-of-fact kind of way. She had managed to struggle free and get away, but she had never told her parents for fear of their reaction. Allitt claimed that Kevin had returned to Corby Glen and followed her home from the Fighting Cocks. She had been so alarmed, she told Steve, that she had asked the landlord and one of the regulars – a man with plenty of muscle – to escort her home.

Steve felt so sorry for his new girl. How could anyone do such a thing? It never crossed his mind that Allitt had made up the whole wretched story. Several years later he finally discovered the truth.

Kevin Fowler had long forgotten his brief encounter with Beverley Allitt.

He had been a boy of seventeen when they had twice been out together drinking in a foursome. Now, six years later, he read in the paper that she had been charged with murdering four children at Grantham and Kesteven Hospital. It was hard to believe because Allitt had seemed 'such an ordinary girl, plain, and a bit dull'.

Their relationship had fizzled out before it had even started. They had never kissed or held one another, but suddenly Kevin began to hear talk that Allitt claimed he had tried to rape her.

'I couldn't believe it when I heard what she'd been saying. She had been putting it round that I had been walking her home, gone behind a tree for a widdle, come at her from behind with a knife, and tried to rape her. She was supposed to have fought me off.

'At first I was upset and went to see a solicitor. I couldn't understand why anyone could make up such a lie. I have never owned a knife, never mind used one to attack a girl. I have always had my share of the girls without that kind of thing. I wouldn't mind if it had been a great big love affair, but we only went out a couple of times for a drink. We'd meet in a foursome at 8pm. We'd have a few drinks at the pub in Corby Glen, and me and my mate would leave Bev and her pal at around 11pm.

'I can only think she made up the story to make people feel sorry for her. She must have a screw loose to do something like that.'

Allitt celebrated her eighteenth birthday on 4 October and Steve spent £15 buying her a Sad Sam, a floppy-eared toy dog, to add to the collection she had at home. He had expected a show of affection but, again, her reaction had been to smile and turn away. Steve recalls: 'She didn't even give me a kiss when I handed her the present.' It was three months before Steve was allowed to meet his girlfriend's family.

'When I finally got introduced to them we got on great. Her dad was a real joker, always going on about lazy roadworkers and how we used to go round digging holes, then filling them in again.

They made me feel so welcome I sometimes would stay for my dinner and tea on a Sunday. Donna, Bev's older sister, lived in Grantham; Alison her younger sister was still at home. Darren, her brother, was only fourteen and they were smashing people.'

Their first few weeks and months together were nearly always happy and it wasn't long before Steve began to suspect he was falling in love.

'Bev used to laugh a lot, we'd do daft things together and really enjoy it. One night it had been raining really heavy and we went out in a four-some in my car. There's a country lane not far from Corby Glen, where you have to ford a stream, and this night it was like a river. I just put my foot down, the water was deeper than the car and we started floating.

'There was water pouring in through the doors. All we could do was drift to the other bank. It was hilarious, we were all in fits, Bev included.'

Even though they had been going steady only a few short months Steve wondered if the relation-ship might lead to marriage. But, in the event, it was Allitt who popped the question as they walked through Corby Glen on their way to meet friends for a night out. She suddenly stopped, turned to Steve and asked him bluntly: 'Do you fancy getting married?'

Steve was taken aback – the question had come out of the blue – but, instinctively, he said 'Yes' straight away. Then he listened as Allitt laid down her terms and conditions. There was no hurry to hold the wedding. Allitt announced they would get married in two or three years time when they'd saved up enough money to settle down.

Steve was jubilant and couldn't wait to present his fiancée with a ring as a token of his love. He went to Grantham and spent £40 at the Argos catalogue store buying Beverley a gold band for her engagement finger. Steve's mother was so delighted she threw a little party to celebrate.

Allitt began collecting household possessions for her bottom drawer and bought a pretty set of flowered crockery called Eternal Beau in readiness for the day when they would be together.

She was the dominant partner, she nearly always got her own way but, when she crashed her fiancé's Ford Escort, the accident was to cause Steve to question her honesty for the first time.

'She didn't have a licence, I knew I was risking it when she asked me if she could drive. We were on the back roads, it was 8pm at night and I had said OK. But she went round a corner too fast, skidded and crashed into a tree. The car was only just driveable. The front end was so badly damaged I had to scrap it.

'I gave Bev a hug and said: "Don't worry about it." I didn't see any reason to lie about it, but she said I had got to tell her dad I'd been driving. She also suggested that we say it had happened near Corby Glen when really we'd been miles and miles away near Stamford. I couldn't understand why we couldn't tell the truth to her family.'

Soon Steve discovered Allitt's love of children; she would take him babysitting.

'She was really keen to get a nursing job. She said she liked looking after children, she loved them and wanted to go into child nursing. I remember going babysitting one night and this little girl, about nine months old, woke up crying. Bev went upstairs, got her back to sleep and she didn't panic one bit. She told me she wanted a couple of kids of her own when she was ready.'

Steve was by now discovering that his fiancée had no appetite for making love. He had hoped it would be a passionate affair, but it was not to be. In two and a half years together they would never share the same bed, and their sexual encounters were brief and unhappy. They would make love at her home when her parents were out, normally about once a month and sometimes not as often as that.

Steve said: 'I decided that Bev didn't like sex much at all. Bev never took her clothes off in front of me. I don't suppose you can call what happened making love. We had sex and there's a difference. When Bev said it was over, then it was over and she used to tell me to stop. She would make me stop and I just took it because I was in love. Each time it only lasted five minutes at the most. She would normally say: "Get off – you're hurting me." '

But Steve remained besotted and was content to let Allitt lay down the rules.

'One month we had sex three times at her house. It was a record for us. The earth didn't exactly move but I thought it was an honour to have sex with her. Even so, she never really gave much of herself to me.'

What was to bring a huge smile to her face, however, was the moment she finally won the promise of a job interview at Grantham Hospital at the beginning of 1988. She wasn't nervous at the prospect, just excited and totally confident the job would be hers.

When the news came that she was successful Allitt was thrilled. But Steve found it hard to share her joy when she told him she intended to leave Corby Glen and move into the nurses' home across the road from the hospital to avoid having to travel sixteen miles a day to Grantham and back. Heartbroken by the announcement Steve recalls: 'We'd been seeing each other every single day and I was really upset at the thought of us only meeting at the weekends. But I was head over heels in love so I said OK.'

Allitt passed her driving test not long after starting work at the hospital and Steve, anxious to do anything for his fiancée, agreed she could borrow his car to drive there each week.

He had spent £1000 replacing the Escort she had written off with an eyecatching silver-and-red Vauxhall Chevette; Allitt's grandfather had loaned him most of the money.

Their weekends together were often stormy and they quarrelled when Allitt spent hours with her head stuck inside medical textbooks studying for her exams.

Allitt wouldn't give Steve her telephone number at the nurses' home so he could call her during the week. In the end he would give her £5 worth of 10p pieces each week in the hope that she would call him. 'Sometimes she wouldn't bother, even though I'd given her the money, and I'd just sit there by the phone waiting and waiting.'

He couldn't understand either why Allitt also refused to let him hold her hand when they were out together in public. Steve was hurt, tortured by the fear that she might be ashamed of their love. He wanted the world to know how much he felt about Bev. Why didn't she feel the same? It was becoming a bleak existence for the bewildered village boy as he endured nights of loneliness and weekends of arguments and violence with his fiancée.

Steve admitted: 'She used to hit me quite a lot and I just had to take it. The arguments were silly, but she'd end up thumping me in the face with her fist. Once she gave me a black eye and it turned all yellowy green. When I told the lads at work that Bev had walloped me they all laughed.

'I'm around 6ft 2ins, I weigh around twelve and a half stones, but she could impose her will on me. She could get what she wanted any time and she did it with other people. Bev can manipulate people.'

Allitt became busy revising for her exams, restricting their time together even more; there was more disappointment when she announced she needed a break and was going away on holiday.

Steve asked: 'Where are we going?'

But Allitt said she had already made up her mind

to go away with a young nurse at the hospital.

Steve said: 'I was jealous. There we were, going steady, and she was telling me she was going away for a fortnight to Spain with another girl. It was awful and I couldn't work out why she was going with her, and not me. There were arguments but in the end I gave in.'

Before Allitt flew off on holiday she told Steve not to drive their car while she was away. She didn't even want it moved. To make sure he complied she even put chalk marks on the tyres and recorded the mileage. 'She said she'd know if I moved it. I thought it was a very odd thing to do, putting chalk on the tyres. I did move it just once while she was away. I drove a few miles, then I put it back in exactly the same spot where she'd left it, making sure the chalk was in the same place. When she got back she accused me of doing 100 miles and we had another row about it.'

Steve had to wait until they had been going out for a year before she finally agreed they could go away on holiday together to a seaside chalet near Great Yarmouth. The girl from the Fighting Cocks would join them with her boyfriend, making up a foursome. But a fortnight before they were to leave, she broke up with her boyfriend and Steve finished up taking both girls away on his own.

He had been expecting to sleep with Allitt but he found she was in no mood for romance. As soon as they arrived at the chalet she announced she would be sharing a room with her girlfriend, rather than with Steve.

'I couldn't believe it, but Bev said it wouldn't be fair on her pal if we slept together, even though the girl said she didn't mind being by herself. Bev insisted she had to keep her company and I finished up on my own. They slept in single beds in the other room. I didn't like it, but there didn't seem to be anything I could do about it.

'One night we were getting ready to go out and Bev came rushing out of the bathroom holding her thumb. She said she'd got it stuck in the tap getting washed. It was red raw so we rushed her to the hospital. We were there until 2am. It was broken and they had to plaster it up. But afterwards I got to thinking what an incredible thing to happen and I decided she'd done it deliberately to be the centre of attention. Bev always had to be the centre of attention.'

Steve was growing increasingly concerned at his sweetheart's strange behaviour and he was shocked when she began holding her girlfriend's hand in the street.

'I thought it was a joke when she started holding her girlfriend's hand, but it went on for two or three days. She started walking like a fella, too. I was getting worried. I asked her friend if she thought Bev had turned queer, and she was worried too. When I asked Bev about it she said she was only joking, but it made me wonder.'

Their stormy love affair continued in spite of his pointed questioning. Allitt persuaded him to grow a moustache. Even though he hated the idea, he complied. 'She reckoned I looked gormless with-

out one. I didn't like the idea one bit, but I stood it
for six or seven months because I was prepared to
do anything to please her. When I shaved it off
eventually she played hell.'

Allitt wasn't particularly interested in how she
looked. She never wore make-up, only studs in her
ears, and spent money only on jeans, jumpers and
sweat-shirts.

But suddenly she decided she was overweight
and began working out, insisting that Steve
needed to shed some flab, too. She would come
home from the hospital and tell her fiancé to do
100 sit-ups. 'I wasn't fat. I really should have told
her to get stuffed, but I even started working out at
the keep-fit classes at the school in the village on a
Tuesday night to keep her happy.'

One night, relaxing at the pub, she talked about
her work and made an astonishing claim.

Steve recalls: 'She was working with the old
people in the geriatric ward and she said the
old blokes would try and grab the nurses and it
wasn't very nice. There was me and her friend
there, and she talked about drugs and said sometimes they would help the old people on their way.

'I don't know whether she meant she had been
doing things herself, but she said they didn't tell
the families what was going on. I didn't like what
she was saying and I told her so.'

Despite everything, Steve was still hoping to
make Allitt his wife, but started to doubt if it would
ever happen.

'I was keen to get married but, whenever I asked

when it was going to happen, Bev would put it off and put it off.'

Their first holiday together had been a miserable affair but Steve felt sure things would be better when they arranged to go away again, this time to Tenerife, with a nurse from the hospital and her boyfriend, Andy Smith.

The four of them each paid £300 to share a self-catering apartment. They flew from East Midlands airport in mid October 1989, in high spirits, determined to enjoy their fortnight in the sun. But, as they arrived at the apartment, Allitt announced once more that she would not be sleeping with her fiancé, just as she had refused to do a year earlier at Great Yarmouth. This time she said she would be sharing a room with her friend from the hospital.

Steve was stunned by the news. Almost naïvely he had expected a fortnight's romance, even passion: after all they were engaged to be married. He had imagined Andy would share a bedroom with his girlfriend and he would be next door with Bev.

'But Bev told me she would be sharing a room instead with the other girl just to keep her company. She told me this in front of Andy and the nurse.'

Steve thought he would try to make the best of it. 'I threw Beverley in the pool half a dozen times to have some fun, but she hated getting wet.' At the end of the first week Steve's patience was running out. He felt Allitt was ignoring him, and spending more and more time with her room-mate. Instead of passionate romance there were passionate arguments with Allitt still refusing to hold her fiancé's hand when they went out together.

One furious row ended with Allitt attacking Steve with her nails, badly scratching the left side of his face. In the fracas he stuck out a leg to try and fend her off. Afterwards, Steve rushed from the apartment, frightened that he had hurt Allitt, and began crying beside the pool.

'I told the nurse that I loved Bev and she must have told her what I'd said. I was crying by the pool when Bev came out and she burst out crying at the sight of me. It was the only time it ever happened, the only time she ever showed any real emotion. She turned to me and said: "Why didn't you tell me you loved me?" I couldn't understand it because I'd been telling her almost non-stop for two years that I loved her. I asked her to leave me alone to calm down.'

Later the unhappy boyfriends, in despair at the way the girls were spending so much time together, commiserated with one another.

Back home Allitt agreed to let her fiancé join her at discos at the hospital social club where he could meet her friends at the nurses' home for the first time. But rather than dance with her fiancé, or even sit talking, Allitt preferred the company of the other nurses. Steve felt he was being ignored. 'She was treating me like I didn't exist.'

Steve, still desperately in love, decided to call Allitt's bluff and announced he wanted to end their engagement. He broke the news as they sat watching TV at her parents' home. Bev's mother and father were out but her younger sister, Alison, was there. 'I was fed up with Bev not showing me any love. I said I wanted to finish with her.

'I said I was going, but Bev slammed the door, tore at my hair and said: "You're not going anywhere." She grabbed my hair and dragged me on to the floor. I was on my knees and shouting, "Get off – let me go." She had upset me so much I was crying. Alison stopped the fighting and said Bev ought to leave me alone.'

They decided to keep going but it was not to last. Out of the blue, in the spring of 1990, Allitt phoned Steve at his home in Corby Glen and said she had decided it was over.

A year later the police arrived unexpectedly at Steve's door, wanting to ask him some questions. He thought it was about an accident he had had driving a lorry at work, so when they asked: 'Do you know why we're here?' he said, yes, it must be about the accident.

But the officers wanted to know about Beverley Allitt. 'I couldn't understand why they would be interested in her. I said, "What's she done?" They told me it was about the misuse of some drugs at the hospital.'

11. 'Help Me!'

David Thorpe and Ruth Lindsey run a private
investigation agency called City Life, based in
Grantham. They were friends of Peter and Sue
Phillips. David, a big man who wore his hair in a
pony-tail, was nicknamed 'Columbo' by Peter after
the scruffy TV detective; his partner, a short attractive girl in her twenties, with long, dark hair and a
round face, is diabetic and takes insulin every day.
This fact was to prove important when they began
to question Nurse Beverley Allitt.

  They were usually employed checking on way-
ward partners in divorce cases and working under-
cover for local solicitors. Suddenly they found
themselves thrust into the middle of a major police
investigation into attempted murder on a children's
ward. Peter and Sue were convinced that they
could help and that, given time, the private-eyes
would be able to prove that Beverley had been
wrongly accused. If it cost money to find the
evidence, then they were quite prepared to pick
up the bill. After all, Allitt was a firm friend and
they were in no doubt that she had saved Katie's
life.

  The nurse seemed delighted that someone

wanted to help her and returned to the Phillips's house for a first meeting with David and Ruth in the evening of 13 June.

The investigators had known Peter and Sue for about a year and had been visiting one night when Becky had fallen ill. They had shared the despair over her death and, knowing what the family had been through, they were only too willing to lend a hand.

Peter explained that he wanted them to investigate the allegations because he felt not enough was being done to defend Beverley. David, clutching a black notebook in which he had recorded the conversation, recalled: 'When we met Beverley, it was awkward at times. We started by putting together background information and then we did a character analysis of her. We were testing out what was going on. We talked for about an hour. She was totally lost. She might as well have been in a different country, speaking a different language. Peter and Sue were trying to comfort her.'

Ruth and David were well aware that the Phillips were convinced that their friend had been falsely accused.

Ruth said: 'She had been questioned by the police under arrest and given police bail. When we saw her, she was like a frightened rabbit. But she was trusted as a friend by Peter and Sue and was going to be godmother to Katie.'

David tried to spell out to Allitt just how serious the situation could be for her. He knew that there had been talk of Allitt being charged by the police.

'But we ran into problems with Bev straight-away. Sometimes she would talk to you and then would forget what she had said. She said she had got a poor memory. She couldn't remember basic hospital routines. Vital things like where the fridge was in the ward, where the controlled drugs cabinet was and who had the keys. She couldn't remember even who she had spoken to.

'She would remember silly, pointless things which, if she was suffering from shock, I thought she would not have remembered. She remembered going to a car-boot sale, one Sunday, with her friend Tracy. She remembered what happened there.

'Yet when I mentioned the following day, when she was at work, she could only remember starting the day. When it came to general day-to-day stuff, like what time she took lunch, she wasn't sure. She wasn't sure what time she usually did things. She wasn't sure about anything. She said her lunchbreak was anything between 11.30 and 2pm which is quite a long time-span.

'We began to wonder whether she was in a form of delayed shock, generally bewildered.'

They began to do a form of 'psychological examination', a DIY test that they had developed in their work as private detectives. They were trying to see if Allitt was telling lies or whether she had forgotten the truth through panic and shock.

'It could have been panic. Most people react in an odd sort of way and you don't know what to expect from different people.'

They gave her a short oral test, not telling her what they were trying to do. It was a test they had developed, using a series of set questions; they were looking for specific responses. 'We were trying to build up a character analysis.

'The first test lasted about an hour and we decided there was no sign of shock at all. She was very calm, a bit tense.

'In training I studied clinical psychology and I needed to find the truth. I told her in front of Peter and Sue that if I found she was guilty I would nail her. I didn't notice any reaction from her when I said that. She said she had nothing to fear, she had not done anything.

'We asked straight out: "Did you do it?" She said: "No I did not." That was as forceful as she got. She was so calm. Nothing I said was going to bother her.

'I wasn't intimidating in the way I was told the police were when they questioned her.'

David left the meeting with the impression that Allitt was holding back and not telling them something; he didn't know what this could be. David and Ruth discussed her answers and studied her reactions.

David said: 'We have a large board where we put all the answers down. We had asked her a lot of questions about the general routine on the ward and also about her relationship with the rest of the staff. And we asked her opinion of the rest of the staff, her opinion about the doctors.

'I asked her about one child she had found who

had turned blue. She had come rushing out with the child. She remembered going into the room (but she couldn't say why she had gone in) and she recalled coming out. Then she remembered going back in there afterwards and she noticed there was a discolouration in the child. She remembered rushing out with the child and we were told she had shouted "Crash" as she came out.

'But she did not remember that.

'We asked her why she had looked into the room, on the second occasion, because the child was not under close observation. She said she looked in because she liked children.'

They asked her about the layout of the cubicles. She was so unsure that she had to ask Sue Phillips.

'I asked her simple questions about what was in a particular room, what it was set out like and she couldn't tell me. She couldn't remember.

'I wanted her to think about actual incidents. For instance, I asked her which side of the bed was the child's head. Was the head pointing to the left or the right? She couldn't remember.

'But if you go into a room and pick up a child, I felt she should remember, but she couldn't even remember the position of the bed.

'There were just mental blocks. Over the next hour and a half, there were more and more mental blocks of a similar nature. She couldn't remember obvious details. A nurse has a particular routine but Bev couldn't remember it.'

Allitt's first meeting with the private detectives

lasted about three hours. They arranged to meet again the following evening at the modern, semi-detached house in Grantham which she shared with Tracy. They arrived with a bottle of wine 'to ease the situation'.

Ruth recalled: 'When we turned up Bev was quite friendly. I think that was her nature, not because of anything else.'

David said: 'I asked her a question about insulin. Ruth is diabetic so we already had a good knowledge of it.

'We gave her the needle and we asked Beverley to show us the actual amount that would have been given to the children. I asked her to do it twice. I wanted her to show us the amount that was supposed to have been injected. It had to be a guess because the amount the police were talking about was ridiculous. It was a massive amount. I wanted to see myself what it looked like.

'She was very fumbly and had to ask Tracy, who was also a nurse, how to do it. In the end Tracy took it off Bev and showed what it would take. Bev had done it before at Pete and Sue's and she had not had a problem. But the second time she began to show anxiety. The amount we had asked her to measure out was the amount the police had told her was used.

'Tracy would answer the questions for her and Bev would correct her, until it got to the point where we might as well have asked Beverley and got the answers from Tracy. If Beverley got it wrong, Tracy would correct her. Bev actually turned round and said to us: "I am known for having a very bad memory."

'The meeting went on for a long time and, at one stage, Tracy told us she thought the house had been bugged. I offered to do a sweep of the place to check but her solicitor, John Kendall, told us not to because he said it would seem that Bev had got something to hide.'

David and Ruth asked Allitt whether she had ever had a spare-time nursing job.

'We needed to know whether she had ever been working anywhere else, but she didn't say. She sort of sketched over it. Much later we found out from Sue that she had been working in an old people's home.

'You are not supposed to work for anyone else when you are a full-time nurse, but Sue told us that Bev had walked on to the hospital ward one night wearing the uniform of the British Nursing Association, the nursing agency. They've got an office in Grantham. It's a totally different outfit to the hospital's uniform and, if the management or even the sister had seen her, she would have been sacked.

'But Sue said Bev didn't seem to care. She said she had to work there for the money. You could have knocked us down with a feather. There had been absolutely no intention on Bev's part to tell us that she'd got another job.

'Then, on 15 June, there was a story in the *Sun* about the hospital and the enquiry. We heard it on the radio as well. Bev and Tracy upped and left and we got a call to say they would let us know where she was staying.'

Ruth and David began tramping the streets of Grantham and surrounding villages, knocking on doors, visiting nurses at home and asking them what they knew about Allitt and the case of Paul Crampton.

David said: 'The police questioned another girl – an eighteen-year-old student nurse. We wanted to talk to her, too, but we were told to leave her alone because the police had hammered her to such a degree she was having problems. They accused her of being an accomplice.'

Detective Superintendent Clifton's reaction after questioning Nurse Beverley Allitt was to double the size of his enquiry team to twenty-four. This gave him the manpower to examine every other death and suspicious illness in great detail. He was totally convinced that he was on to something, but he still didn't know quite what it was.

Officers were paired together and allocated individual cases to investigate. Each pair began to identify with a particular family and to look at what it could say. They also looked at what various nurses could remember. Each of these pairs investigated its own child and used a police computer system called Holmes to store and evaluate the information that was gathered.

Supt Clifton considered that the answer to many of his questions might be hidden in blood samples taken from the children. The problem was that, by a strange quirk of the National Health Service, they had been sent to eight different laboratories all over the Midlands and the north of England for different analysis. Without the samples, the whole investigation would flounder.

Detective Inspector Neil Jones, who had joined the team, began tracking down the samples. He found the sample of Becky Phillips's blood tucked away in the basement of the City Hospital at Nottingham. He found other crucial samples stored in a fridge in a public health laboratory in Leeds; there were samples still totally unchecked in Sheffield and Boston. Soon he had a small blood bank of his own to send for analysis; then he anxiously awaited the results.

The first to come back was that of twin Becky Phillips who had died at her home just twelve hours after being discharged from hospital; she had been recorded as a 'cot death' victim. The tests on her blood revealed that she, too, had been given an enormous overdose of insulin. Her level, which was not as high as that of Paul Crampton, was recorded as 9660, compared with a normal level of just 4.

The discovery explained Becky's symptoms of the night she'd died. Those twisted contortions on her face, those rolling eyes and piercing screams had been the fits and convulsions caused by a hypoglycemic attack. The massive insulin overdose had sent her body sugar levels plummeting, eventually to kill her.

Each time she'd been fed, she had improved

briefly as her body extracted sugar from the milk. But the relief could only have been temporary, and death inevitable, without a huge input of glucose like the one that had saved Paul Crampton.

Supt Clifton now had the evidence that at least two children, neither of them diabetics, had been poisoned, both with huge amounts of insulin.

After Becky Phillips the detectives began to take an even closer look at the deaths of Claire Peck, Liam Taylor and Timothy Hardwick, all of whom had died on Ward Four in the space of sixty days. They wanted to know whether they, too, had been poisoned, possibly with insulin like Becky Phillips and Paul Crampton.

There was no problem finding a blood sample from Claire, the last to die, because one had been taken during the course of the marathon one-and-a-half-hour unsuccessful attempt to save her. The blood had been sent away for testing.

The result produced a real shock. There was no trace of insulin in Claire's blood. Instead, it was found to contain in excess of 16 millimoles per litre of potassium chloride, more than twice the amount needed to kill her.

Potassium chloride, one of the most lethal poisons known to man, is naturally present in everyone's blood. The average level is about three or four millimoles per litre of blood; this rises dramatically after death. It is readily available in solution in hospitals all over the world, including Ward Four at the Grantham and Kesteven Hospital, for the routine treatment of patients whose potassium chloride level drops, producing symptoms of vomiting and gastro-enteritis. Too much potassium chloride causes the heart to relax and then simply stop beating.

To Supt Clifton and his team of detectives in Grantham it was becoming clear that they were on the trail of a determined killer. He was convinced that Claire must have been injected with the drug.

But how many more children had suffered like Claire, Paul and Becky?

And although he was gathering a mass of medical evidence he had still not found anyone who had seen the killer at work on Ward Four. What Supt Clifton needed was a witness, possibly a parent, relative or, better still, a nurse who had seen a child being given a fatal injection; someone who had seen the killer, if there was one, still holding the 'smoking syringe' like a gun after a shooting.

Every nurse, doctor, ward orderly, porter – anyone who might have had access to Ward Four – had been questioned, often several times, without success. Supt Clifton and his team of medical advisers, sifting through the records of every patient on Ward Four, turned the clock back to the death of Liam Taylor, the first to die.

A detective said: 'We knew that he suffered an infarction of the heart which we were told is unknown in babies. An infarction is where the muscles of the heart die, but you just don't hear of infarctions in infants, it's absolutely unknown.

'We were told it could have been caused by a

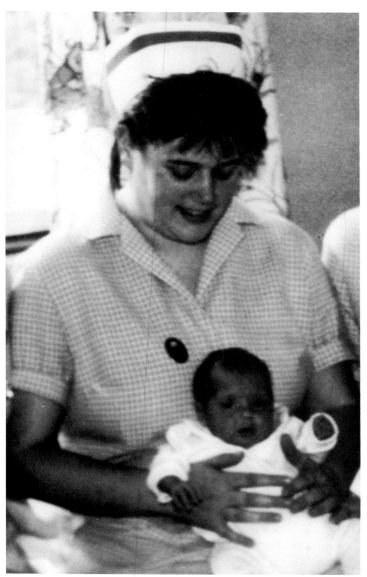

Nurse Beverley Allitt on Ward Four holding Katie Phillips

Liam Taylor ('Pudding Pants')
and his father Chris Taylor

David and Sue Peck with
daughter Claire

Claire Peck

Beverley Gail Allitt in custody outside Grantham Magistrates Court

Nurse Allitt holding Becky Phillips on Ward Four

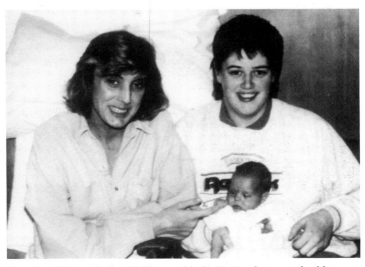

Beverley Allitt with Sue Phillips and baby Katie photographed by father Peter

Timothy Hardwick – 'My special boy'

Timothy's mother Margaret Hardwick arriving at the inquest in Grantham with husband Robert

Twins Patrick and Anthony Elstone

Beverley Allitt on holiday

Detective Superintendent
Stuart Clifton

Hospital chaplain, Reverend
Ian Shelton

Peter and Sue Phillips with surviving twin Katie

Beverley Allitt by the swimming pool on holiday in Tenerife with
friend Tracy Jobson (*left*)

Allitt's friend Tracy Jobson

Tracy's mother Eileen with Jack

Fiancé Steve Biggs – Allitt's one true love

Schoolgirl Beverley Allitt on a sponsored bike ride in Corby Glen with a friend

Bradley Gibson with mother Judith and father Stephen

Photographs: *The Sun*/Mark Tattersall

variety of things, either by asphyxiation, or by insulin or potassium, nobody could tell us which one for certain.'

The police knew that there had been controversy about the cause of his death right from the beginning when his father had expressed his concern and paediatrician Dr Nanayakkara had written to the coroner challenging the cause of his death. The doctor had disagreed with the result of the post mortem. He did not suggest that death was deliberate; he simply disputed the given cause.

The police team, however, was now convinced that Liam's death had been such an unexpected occurrence that something *must* have happened, but they still didn't know what.

Tests in the case of handicapped Timothy Hardwick, the second to die, revealed an abnormally high potassium reading, well above the fatal level. The cause of his death had been recorded as 'cerebral palsy and epilepsy' but, when children die of an epileptic fit, it causes a brain reaction. Further tests showed no signs of this in Timothy's case. Supt Clifton was again convinced that the post-mortem result was wrong.

He decided to call a meeting of minds – a gathering of all the experts from the police and medical teams – to decide his next move. Appropriately, the chosen venue was a conference room across the road from the hospital.

Those who gathered were eminent insulin experts, Professor Marks and Dr David Teal, from the University of Surrey; distinguished paediatric pathologist and 'cot death' specialist Professor John Emery from Sheffield Children's Hospital; paediatric consultant Derek Johnstone and paediatric pathologist Dr David Fagin; and Professor David Hull from the Queen's Medical Centre, Nottingham.

They were joined by representatives of the Area Health Authority, together with the Grantham Hospital paediatricians, Dr Porter and Dr Nanayakkara, and representatives of the hospital management.

Several senior police officers, including Assistant Chief Constable Alan Goldsmith, were there, together with representatives of the Crown Prosecution Service. Barrister John Goldrick, who would ultimately consider the evidence, also attended.

The story was by now becoming a big news item. The conference room was besieged by reporters, photographers and five TV camera crews long before the meeting was due to begin on the afternoon of Tuesday, 2 July.

Meanwhile, a drama was taking place a hundred miles away in the air above Guildford.

Professor Marks, a vitally important participant, had warned Supt Clifton that he would be late for the 2pm start because he had another meeting to attend which would not finish until midday.

Professor Marks was to be flown to Grantham in a hired Cessna.

It should have been a simple exercise but it almost ended in disaster.

As he took off from Guildford, the professor's door flew open, terrifying the valued specialist who, fortunately, was strapped in with his seatbelt. It also horrified Detective Inspector Neil Jones, sitting in the back seat, who feared the prosecution case was about to go literally out of the door. They managed to slam the flapping door shut in mid-air and carried on in time to make the meeting.

The discussions were expected to go on for three hours, but it was five and a half hours later before they ended. Supt Clifton started by delivering a presentation to the gathering, explaining his findings so far. He was followed by the experts. As the meeting continued there was growing realisation amongst them all that the epidemic of sudden collapses and deaths on Ward Four was no accident. Allitt spent the afternoon waiting for news in her solicitor's office a mile away, fearing that the conference would end with her arrest. Her solicitor went to the police station to be ready for possible charges.

But the meeting ended with the experts deciding to prepare new and detailed reports reappraising the cases one by one; then a file could be sent to the Director of Public Prosecutions who would decide what further action to take. It would be many weeks before a final decision would be made.

The detectives and some of the medical experts adjourned for further discussion to the Blue Pig, a move that almost wrecked arrangements to take Professor Marks back to Guildford by patrol car.

Uniformed road traffic officers, who had been given the job of driving him home, combed the town looking for their VIP passenger. When, finally, they arrived at the Blue Pig they burst in so quickly that they silenced the entire pub. Regulars said they thought they'd been caught up in a police raid.

12. 'Becky was Murdered'

Sue Phillips was just about to go shopping when Allitt arrived at the house. She brought with her a letter from the police saying that her bail period, due to end in two weeks, would be extended, due to further investigation.

Peter Phillips, who was still doing all he could to help Allitt prove her innocence, comforted her with the view that the police obviously hadn't found anything in their investigations.

Looking relieved, Allitt offered to take Sue shopping in her car, just the two of them.

As they arrived in the town centre, busy with crowds of shoppers preparing for the weekend ahead, Allitt turned to Sue nervously and asked: 'Are you sure you want to walk round town with me? People may see us. A lot of people are not talking to me any more. They may take it out on you'.

Sue told her not to talk rubbish.

But, as they walked past Marks and Spencers, they spotted another nurse from the hospital walking towards them – and Sue watched in amazement as they saw the nurse deliberately duck round a corner, quite obviously intent on avoiding them. Sue felt even more sorry for Allitt.

The suspended nurse was still a regular visitor to the Phillips household; Sue and Peter were not aware that detectives were, by then, investigating the cases of Becky and Katie.

Saturday, 15 June, was an awful day. The rain was cascading down when Allitt arrived at the front door.

Katie was 'playing up', Sue recalls, as Allitt joined the family for lunch. Afterwards, Allitt offered to take Katie for a walk in her buggy while Sue cleared up the lunch. It was raining outside, Sue questioned the wisdom of the venture but Allitt countered: 'Don't worry, it will give you a rest.'

She got out the buggy, placed Katie in it, attached her protective hood, then dashed to the car in the pouring rain to get her own coat, and then set off.

She'd been suspended from duty, accused by the police of attempting to murder Paul Crampton and was now dashing off into the rain with baby Katie. Both Sue and Peter Phillips were so utterly convinced of her innocence, so sure the police were wrong, that they didn't give it a second thought.

Five short minutes later Allitt was back, bursting through the door 'like a rocket'. She left the buggy in the hall and then, huffing and puffing as she tried to get her breath after sprinting down the road, she told them to telephone for a doctor straightaway because she was certain Katie was about to go into convulsions at any minute.

She told them: 'Get a doctor. You must get a doctor.'

Sue heard Katie crying and ran to the buggy to find her face was 'as red as a postbox', and she was sweating.

Oh no! Could this be Becky all over again?

Allitt was, by now, pleading with them – just get a doctor.

But the Phillips had no telephone of their own. Their car-valeting business had collapsed with the arrival of the twins. Sue had been unable to work and, amidst the ensuing financial chaos, they had just had their telephone disconnected. Allitt volunteered to drive Sue round to her parents, Bill and Hazel Garrett, to phone their GP.

The woman locum doctor responded so quickly that she pulled up outside the house at the same time as Allitt and Sue arrived back.

The doctor decided to take no chances and sent Katie back to Ward Four. Once again, suspecting nothing, Sue and Peter thanked Allitt for her swift actions. They felt that the nurse had done the right thing in reacting so quickly to the potential emergency. Peter recalls thinking she was 'a real brick'.

Katie recovered rapidly in hospital, though the cause for her relapse was never detected.

But, while she was in hospital, Peter used the opportunity to speak to nurses during his visits, trying to gather any evidence that would help Allitt's defence.

His activities, however, infuriated the police

who were in the middle of a delicate murder investigation. Peter's DIY detective work, although
well intentioned, was becoming a nuisance. They
even considered giving him an official warning
to 'back off' or end up being arrested himself.
If the senior detectives involved in the investigation were in any doubt about how strongly the
Phillips felt about the situation, it was rudely
spelled out to them when two detectives called at
their house on Monday, 17 June. By then, the
police had received the results of the blood tests
on Becky.

The two CID officers arrived at the Phillips's
home at 9am to ask Peter and Sue to accompany
them to Grantham police station to see Detective
Superintendent Clifton. Peter, by now wound-up
like a watchspring by the obvious unfairness (as he
saw it) of the police suspicions, couldn't hold back
his anger.

'If he wants to f.... well see us, he can f.... well
come up here!' he snapped. He went on: 'Look, we
have told you lot everything we know about Paul
Crampton and we just don't want any more.'

The police officers explained that there was
something else that Supt Clifton wanted to tell
them for himself. Peter demanded to know what
they meant by 'something else'.

Then came the bombshell.

It wasn't about Paul Crampton at all, they told
him. It was about Becky and Katie.

The mention of their two babies' names was
enough.

Sue and Peter went to Grantham police station, sitting together in the back of the unmarked police car, hardly daring to look at each other, let alone speak.

In the first-floor room at the stone-built police station, Supt Clifton was flanked by Detective Chief Inspector Alan Smith, Detective Inspector Neil Jones, Policewoman Jane McGuire and Detective Gerry Thorold.

Softly, the police broke the news. DCI Smith told them that the police had been investigating incidents involving several children. A professor had looked at samples of blood taken from Becky.

He went on: 'We have found something in the blood sample.'

Looking across from his desk, Supt Clifton told them: 'I have to tell you some bad news. We have found insulin in your daughter's blood which measures a level of nearly 10,000.'

Peter asked: 'What does that mean?'

Supt Clifton told them: 'It means your daughter was murdered.'

Sue remembers gazing out of the window at an oak tree, swaying in the breeze; she uttered not a word, her mind a total blank, in a state of shock. Peter reacted differently and began to cry, unable to speak. Neither of them could take in the enormity of what they were being told.

Sue broke the silence: 'Do you know who is doing this?' she asked.

The police chief nodded.

Sue told him she'd spoken to Bev Allitt who had

told them she had been questioned about Paul Crampton.

Supt Clifton told her: 'Yes, but she failed to tell you that we have also interviewed her about both your daughters and other children.'

The penny finally began to drop.

Peter asked: 'What does Bev say?'

The police chief told him: 'Don't worry about her.'

Sue believes they were the last of all the families involved to be told of the police suspicions.

News had already started to leak out to the press and, even as they left the police station, a TV crew was waiting outside. Quietly, they slipped out through a back door.

Alone with their thoughts, they started to look back, churning over in their whirling minds every detail of Becky's death, hunting for clues they might have missed. How, they wondered, could it be true? Sue had never accepted that Becky had died from a 'cot death' because, right from the beginning, she knew it had been nothing like that. But being given the news that Becky had been murdered was like reliving the night she died. It was like her dying all over again, only this was worse.

They were driven straight home by the same two CID officers who had taken the full force of Peter's wrath. Now they were all silent.

Back in the safety of their own four walls, Sue and Peter needed to let the awful news quietly sink in, to come to terms with the mixture of shock and blind anger building up inside them. But yet another unexpected problem was waiting for them.

When they reached home they were greeted on the doorstep by Peter's sixteen-year-old schoolgirl daughter Emma who told them: 'Bev's been here while you were out.' She went on: 'Bev wants to know whether she can stay here with us.'

Allitt had asked her if Sue and Peter had read that morning's newspapers which had printed the story of the police investigation. Emma told her truthfully that they had not. Allitt wanted some-where to hide because eager newspapermen were trying to find her, she said.

Sue and Peter stood in virtual disbelief as Emma told them: 'She wants to put her car in our garage and move in upstairs where they will not find her.' Emma had told her to call back later when Sue and Peter had returned. Sue turned on the kettle to make a much-needed cup of tea. They were both angry and appalled by Allitt's request.

Sue said later: 'I couldn't believe my ears. After what we had just heard from the police, I couldn't take it all in. We had just been told that the police suspected her of poisoning both Becky and Katie, and here she was, asking us to help shelter her in our house.

'Becky was dead and Katie was in hospital and she wanted to move into our house? She wanted us to protect her?'

The two CID officers, who had just driven them home, bluntly told Peter and Sue: 'Just keep her

163

away.' They drove off to find Allitt to tell her not to go back.

She would never set foot in the Phillips' house again.

Beverley Allitt desperately needed somewhere to hide.

She had been turned down by the Phillips and she couldn't use the nurses' home because she had been barred from going anywhere near the Grantham and Kesteven Hospital.

Hotly pursued by newsmen, the young nurse turned for help to Tracy Jobson, her closest friend for two years. The two girls had worked at the same hospital, shared a house, been on holiday together and had rarely been apart. They knew each other almost like sisters.

Tracy, a lean girl with short, dark hair who worked in the intensive care unit at the hospital, had been one of the casualty 'crash team' sent dashing to Ward Four to try to save some of the children. At the same time she had been sharing a rented house with Allitt in Grantham.

Like the rest of the medical staff she never imagined that the children were being deliberately harmed at the hospital where they both worked. There was never anything in Allitt's behaviour to ever make her suspicious.

Trusting her friend entirely, Tracy suggested that she move in with her mother Eileen, and her fifteen-year-old brother, Jonathan, who lived in a terraced house in Orton Goldhay on the outskirts of Peterborough, thirty miles to the south of Grantham. No one surely would think of looking for her there. It was to be a move Mrs Jobson would live to regret for the rest of her days. During her four months as guest of the Jobsons, strange and bizarre incidents began to happen that would first baffle and, eventually, strike an awful note of terror.

It was mid June when Allitt arrived in Orton Goldhay to escape the reporters and TV crews who had gathered in Grantham. Mrs Jobson welcomed her with open arms and treated her like a daughter. Like Tracy, she thought the police had made a ghastly mistake.

The three women spent hours analysing the allegations, trying to prove Allitt's innocence. At one stage Allitt sat down and carefully wrote down on paper details of her every movement on Ward Four on the days when children had been taken ill.

Tracy recalls: 'I used to put it to her: "What have you been doing?" But Bev had it all worked out. I believed her, of course I believed her, I believed what she told me. She would break down, start crying, and say if I didn't believe her she would kill herself. She said it hundreds of times.

'She would look me in the eye and say: "I didn't do it. I had nothing to do with it." And, remember, I didn't work on the ward and had no information about what had gone on there.'

She added: 'People who don't know Bev will never understand how she is so normal, so convincing. She has an answer for absolutely everything. It was difficult to believe that anyone could do this, let alone someone you think you know. She's not an obviously mad person – far from it.'

Mrs Jobson believed her too. She said: 'When she was living here I never once suspected her. Bev is a very bright, clever girl.'

But, just days after Allitt's arrival, odd things began to take place behind the door of Mrs Jobson's neat and smartly decorated home.

Curtains in the bathroom were found with scorch marks where an attempt had clearly been made to set them alight. Then a knife from the kitchen drawer was discovered plunged through the pillow on her bed. Money mysteriously went missing and Mrs Jobson's purse vanished, only to be found later in Allitt's car. Bleach was spilled on the lounge carpet and also on a bed, leaving huge, unrepairable stains. Mrs Jobson's walking stick, left in one room, would vanish and reappear in another part of the house. And a dish moved from a shelf to a settee.

When Allitt was asked about these occurrences, she insisted it was nothing to do with her and tried to suggest that a poltergeist had taken over the house. The strange events suddenly took a more sinister twist when Mrs Jobson's Jack Russell, called Jack, coughed up the obvious remains of two tablets in the back garden. Allitt, who had been alone in the house, had run outside as Mrs Jobson returned from work, to announce: 'Come quickly. Jack's ill.'

Taken in isolation, each event would not have unnerved Mrs Jobson but, as they continued, she became increasingly disturbed by the succession of peculiar happenings.

She recalls: 'It was as though Bev was trying to create dramas. Things like finding a knife through my pillow, that was quite sinister. It was weird. She knew I would find things that she had done. With half the things, she was practically pointing them out if I didn't notice.

'On the night the knife was stuck through the pillow, she shouted to me to come and have a look. I just said "Gosh!" Then I said: "I think this is getting bloody ridiculous."

'But she said she didn't do it, she never did anything.'

For three weeks Jonathan was away, leaving Mrs Jobson alone in the house with Allitt.

'It would just be her and me in the house. She tried to tell me it was Tracy who was doing it but she definitely wasn't. What she didn't realise was that, when a lot of the things happened, there were four or five witnesses in the house and still they continued. The more people here, the more things happened. The bigger the audience, the better it was. It was unreal. She was a performer. Things were happening nearly every single day.

'It was my sister who eventually said: "Enough." She thought my life was in danger.

'She could see it because she wasn't so close to it. Bev had got me to a stage where she had me where she wanted me. You would believe anything rather than believe she was doing those things. She had no reason to do things to me, because I was her friend.

'In the end I knew it was her but I felt I had to catch her, that I couldn't accuse her without proof. We tried for a long time to catch her, but we didn't. We followed her everywhere around the house but never saw her do anything.

'It never once occurred to me, even then, that if she was doing these things here then she could have done the things at the hospital. I honestly felt the reason why she was doing it was because of all the pressure she was under. It was her reaction. She hadn't shown any reaction. She convinced me she was innocent.'

Worse was still to come for the trusting Jobsons.

Allitt, still waiting for the Director of Public Prosecutions to decide whether or not she should be charged with the murders and attempted murders on Ward Four, joined Mrs Jobson and her son, Jonathan, on an outing to the Sunday open-air market at Whittlesey, on the edge of the Fens.

Without warning the healthy schoolboy suddenly collapsed in a heap on the floor.

Mrs Jobson said: 'I thought he was dead. There was no sign of life, not a flicker. I couldn't understand what had happened to him. Bev did absolutely nothing, even though she's a nurse. She was there at the market and I screamed at her to help but she did nothing.

'I took it that she was in shock. She looked like

she was in a state of shock. She looked sort of detached. She'd flicked a switch off.

'By the time I got him to the hospital he was all right again. The doctor said he was sure he'd just fainted. But I knew it wasn't just a faint. I had never seen a faint like that.

'Jonathan and Bev actually made a joke of it afterwards. I remember Jonathan saying something like: "What would the police think of this – you living here and me being taken to hospital?" Jonathan worshipped the ground on which Bev walked. He loved her like a big sister.'

She added: 'We knew he had had a glass of blackcurrant before we went to the market. At the time, nobody thought anything about it. We weren't suspicious at all. Why should we be? All that we were reading in the papers was that children were having insulin or potassium chloride and, to my mind, you would have to be injected, so it never occurred to anybody.'

Mrs Jobson kept quiet about the weird events that had occurred at her house. The police made several attempts to question her at length but they sensed that she was wary of speaking to them, out of loyalty to her daughter's best friend.

Finally, after a family conference, they decided it was time to summon the police.

Relatives were beginning to fear that Mrs Jobson's life might be in danger and a call was made to Grantham police station at around midnight.

Detective Inspector Neil Jones, the man who had

tracked down the blood samples from Ward Four, was despatched to talk to Mrs Jobson in the early hours. He listened in astonishment. The police had imagined that Allitt was living quietly, keeping a low profile, waiting for the decision of the DPP, but what the detective inspector heard opened up a chilling new chapter in the investigation.

So much was said, so much happened during Allitt's four months at Mrs Jobson's home, that it took the police thirty hours to write down her statement. Allitt, driven out of Grantham, now found herself unwelcome and in need of a new hideaway once more. She turned to her parents, Richard and Lillian, in the village of Corby Glen.

They had never doubted their daughter's innocence and were happy to see her return.

Back in her own home her father's employer, wine merchant Jeremy Marshall-Roberts, offered her a job working in his warehouse. Such was their conviction that she was innocent, he and his wife happily agreed to have Allitt back as babysitter for their young children.

The sinister events at the Jobson house gave detectives further suspicions about the state of Allitt's mind.

Some detectives had long believed they were looking for a 'nutter' – someone who outwardly looked normal but who was really mad enough to become the worst woman serial killer in British history.

13. The Motive

Supt Clifton and his team of investigators had wrestled with the one big question – why?

How could anyone kill babies in a hospital? It had seemed impossible, unreal, unthinkable to imagine that it had happened in a corner of rural Lincolnshire. But now he had proof that the children on Ward Four had been poisoned. Again, he asked himself – what, in the name of God, would have made anyone do such an awful thing?

Nurse Allitt, just twenty-three years old, had always showed such a love of children and seemed to have an overwhelming desire to be a good nurse. But he was convinced that there was a secret, hidden side to her mind that had driven her to the depths of evil.

Hospital paediatrician, Dr Nelson Porter, first told Supt Clifton about a condition called Munchausen Syndrome – a chronic form of attention seeking. He'd mentioned it at their first meeting on 1 May. He recalled that paediatricians had been alerted to the danger of mothers seeking attention for themselves by deliberately making their children so ill that they needed hospital treatment.

Dr Porter wondered whether someone suffering from Munchausen Syndrome was to blame for the chain of events on Ward Four. Research also indicated that nurses suffering from the condition could be driven to attack children in their care.

One detective said: 'We hadn't got a clue at the beginning what he was talking about. Some of us asked: "What the hell is Munchausen Syndrome?" It was completely over our heads. It seemed unbelievable that someone in that hospital was so desperate for attention that they were prepared to kill and kill again.

'Perhaps they didn't mean to kill anyone and were just trying to make them ill, but it had just gone too far. Perhaps they wanted to be involved in the drama of trying to save them, then get the praise for helping them to survive from the brink of death.'

But Munchausen Syndrome, they discovered, wasn't a condition of madness defined under the Mental Health Act; it was a personality disorder known to have driven people, almost all of them women, to harm children.

It had been named after an eighteenth-century German baron, Karl Friedrich Hieronymus von Munchausen, a mercenary and gifted story-teller, who would entertain his dinner guests by inventing the most amazing fanciful tales. The condition was first identified in 1951 by Richard Asher, father of actress Jane Asher, who gave it the name of Munchausen Syndrome.

Dr Asher, an eminent physician with a keen

interest in psychological medicine, had become fascinated by the bizarre acting abilities of hospital patients who invented illnesses in order to get attention. He examined why some people actually liked to be admitted to hospital and were able to simulate diseases or make up totally fictitious illnesses in order to get admitted, often travelling from one hospital to another telling weird and wonderful stories of make-believe symptoms. They would have their stories absolutely pat and were brilliantly able to concoct complaints that would be guaranteed to get them treatment.

Twenty-five years later, another group of odd-ball people was identified, those who seek attention for themselves by inducing illnesses in others. Their condition became known as Munchausen Syndrome by Proxy – getting someone else to be ill for them.

Supt Clifton knew from fiancé Steve Biggs how Allitt had deliberately injured her finger by jamming it into a tap. He also knew that she was a regular patient in hospital with what appeared to be self-inflicted injuries.

Supt Clifton's enquiries revealed even more strange aspects of Allitt's past. While she had been living at the nurses' home across the road from the hospital there had been a series of peculiar incidents in the unit of four bedsits where she was staying. Other nurses found excreta smeared on the communal door leading to the four flatlets. That was odd in itself. But then another door was daubed in the kitchen Allitt shared with the other nurses. More was left in their bath. Worse still, the disgusted nurses opened their fridge to find even more excreta lying on a shelf.

Several days later the fire brigade was called when smoke filled the flatlets. The firemen found that a further deposit had been placed under the grill of the cooker which had been switched on and left to burst into flames. Allitt, still in the middle of her training, was never suspected of being the culprit. The police were alerted and an official hospital enquiry undertaken. Everyone agreed that it was a particularly distasteful chain of events but, with no clues, the enquiries led nowhere. The whole matter was finally forgotten.

But when Supt Clifton and his team began to take a close look at Allitt's life they discovered other strange details about her medical history. As a child she had been prone to limb fractures or sprains. School friends remembered Allitt 'always being in bandages'. During her training as a nurse she had been off sick so often her period as a student had to be extended. At one point she had 'injured' her wrist and, when she had ignored medical advice to undergo continuous physiotherapy, the physiotherapist penned a note complaining that Allitt, in her view, was not fit to be a nurse.

It didn't end there. While on police bail Allitt again returned to hospital. She was fitted with a catheter when she apparently developed a urinary problem, but it broke. Allitt was detained in hospital in Peterborough where staff noticed that, during the day, she always appeared well. At night her temperature rose and she became ill. Her breasts were also painful. Later it was suspected that she had deliberately injected her breasts with water using a syringe, probably taken from the nursing station near her bed. It seemed she was trying to focus attention on herself.

The police were told that, with her medical knowledge, Allitt would know that injecting her breasts with water would have the effect of sending her temperature soaring and causing her to be ill. Supt Clifton needed to know if Allitt was suffering from Munchausen Syndrome. Could this be what had driven her to attack the children? He had to understand this rare condition better if it was to stand as a real motive for murder.

Turning to one of Britain's top experts on the condition, Supt Clifton contacted Professor Roy Meadow, head of the Department of Paediatrics and Child Health at St James's University Hospital, Leeds. Professor Meadow had written an article in the *British Medical Journal*, in July 1989, in which he chronicled the symptoms of Munchausen. He had also warned that, among sufferers, were mothers who had targeted their own children.

In many cases, women with Munchausen Syndrome had had some medical training, usually in nursing. They might not have been fully trained to the top level and were likely to be nursing auxiliaries; they could even have left the training before completing the course. All were capable of doing horrific things to children in their care.

Professor Meadow told how sufferers resorted

to 'cunning and dexterity' and were usually 'medically sophisticated'. In Sheffield a mother had been convicted of deliberately feeding her child slug pellets over a period of weeks so that the child ended up fighting for its life in the hospital's intensive care unit.

Experts who examined the bizarre attacks in detail found that a mother often became the life and soul of the hospital ward where her child was being treated. She would look after other children, become friends with other mothers and see herself as an expert on medical matters, often challenging nurses and doctors over the type of treatment.

Professor Meadow wrote: 'For most mothers there is personal gain in terms of status, contacts with helpful nurses, doctors and social workers, financial benefits, contact with other mothers, and a different society in hospital, escape from an unhappy marriage or the capture of an absent husband to share a problem.'

He concluded: 'After talking with many of these mothers my main impression is of their immense selfishness; they are able to do horrific things to children because of their own unhappiness, and to satisfy their own needs. In a minority, particularly those who indulge in suffocation or poisoning, there commonly is envy of, and violence and hatred towards, the abused child.'

The professor gave a simple set of checks for doctors to use when they were suspicious. He suggested that they should secure and verify charts and records, retain and analyse samples – such as blood and urine – for toxicology, increase surveillance, involve the social services and exclude the mother, through legal force if necessary. But his warnings and guidance had been targeted on parents whose children repeatedly suffered from unexplained illness.

In Grantham, the hospital found itself dealing with the virtually uncharted possibility that genuinely ill children were being systematically attacked inside hospital by a nurse.

Supt Clifton decided that, if this case was ever to go to trial, he needed Professor Meadow to be a Crown expert.

The police team was surprised that a nurse could ever dream of harming a patient; they were 'angels' who had dedicated their lives to saving people, not harming them. But around the world nurses had been accused of killing their patients, some in the most horrific circumstances.

In the most bizarre incident nurses at the Las Vegas Sunrise Hospital were accused of running a sweepstake on the time patients would die; one nurse was charged with murder by tampering with life-support systems to increase her chances of winning the bet. The *New York Post* splashed the story over its pages with the headline: 'Angel of Death', adding in smaller type: 'Nurse Accused of Pulling Plug in Lethal Hospital Betting Scandal'. The case shocked and gripped America although the charges were eventually dropped.

In Austria four nurses were charged with killing more than forty patients. The police said they had injected insulin or water into terminally ill patients 'to help them on their way'.

But in an analysis of the British record, the magazine *Nursing Standard* concluded: 'British nurses should feel proud of their sparse, if not spotless, record for murder. Not only do they compare favourably to their foreign counterparts but, unlike their British medical colleagues, they are also noticeably absent from the murderers' hall of fame.

'Convictions of nurses for actual murder – if not attempted murder – of patients are, so far, mercifully unknown.'

The magazine quoted Val Cowie, Director of the Royal College of Nursing's labour relations and legal department, as saying that British nurses did not have a record of killing their patients because 'the notion is so contrary to everything that our profession believes and holds dear. It's difficult to comprehend how a nurse in a nursing role could murder anybody.'

The only exception had been the case of Sister Jessie McTavish who, at the age of thirty-four, was sentenced to life imprisonment for the murder of a patient at Ruchill Hospital, Glasgow, by injecting her with insulin.

She had denied murdering eighty-year-old Miss Elizabeth Lyon, a geriatric patient at the hospital, by injecting her repeatedly with insulin without medical authority or prescription. She was convicted by a majority verdict in the Edinburgh High Court.

But, in February 1975, after spending three

months in prison, Sister McTavish was freed amid emotional scenes when the Court of Appeal quashed her conviction.

One case in particular, however, grabbed the attention of detectives investigating the events on Ward Four.

It was the trial of a young nurse who had been convicted of murdering a fifteen-month-old toddler called Chelsea McClellan with a fatal injection of the drug succinylcholine at a children's clinic on the other side of the Atlantic, in the Texan town of Kerrville in 1981. Nurse Genene Jones was also suspected of poisoning up to fifteen other children when she worked the night shift in the paediatric intensive care unit of a hospital in the nearby city of San Antonio, Texas. All the children had fallen ill on the 3–11pm shift while Jones was on duty; so many youngsters were involved that it became known as the 'Death Shift'.

An internal investigation revealed that one of the nurses was almost certainly attacking the children but, frightened of bad publicity and potential lawsuits, the hospital didn't call in the police to investigate. They removed Jones from the staff and allowed her to start a new job at another clinic with a good recommendation.

Once she'd arrived there, the awful pattern began again; healthy children collapsed with fits, seizures and heart attacks.

Police exhumed Chelsea's body to obtain the vital evidence that she had been poisoned, and Jones was jailed for ninety-nine years in

1984 in the 'Texas Baby Murders' trial.

These events might have passed unnoticed to the team of detectives investigating the attacks on Ward Four had the story of Genene Jones not been recorded in a paperback book called *The Death Shift* which sold all over the world – including Grantham. Detectives discovered that there was a copy of the book in Grantham town library. Two others had been sold in the town.

Could it be, they began to wonder, that this was a copycat killing? Had someone read the book and decided to repeat the Texas Baby Murders in England? After all, Claire Peck was fifteen months old, just like Chelsea McClellan when she died, and one of the other victims who survived was a severely handicapped boy, like Timothy Hardwick. Many others were tiny babies.

A detective was despatched by Supt Clifton with a mission to track down every copy of the book known to be in Grantham and to check out every person who had borrowed it from the library since its publication in 1990. There were rumours that the 448-page red-backed book had been seen on Ward Four. One parent claimed she saw a nurse with a book she thought could be *The Death Shift* under her arm. The police could never establish whether or not that was true, though the book would later become a bestseller in Grantham.

Copies were ordered at the bookshop called Limelight, opposite the Angel and Royal Hotel, by medical staff, policemen and many of the families whose children were at the centre of the investigation. Those involved in the case were fascinated and sickened by the similarities between the Texas case and their own in Grantham. When Chelsea's father, Reed McClellan, heard that the families in Grantham were going through the same ordeal, he sent them a message of support, saying: 'My heart goes out to you. I can only advise you to keep going, keep fighting, because you will get justice in the end.'

What particularly interested the Grantham detectives was the theory that Genene Jones had been driven to kill and attack children because she was suffering from Munchausen Syndrome by Proxy.

The outside world was now taking notice of the events in Grantham and media interest was beginning to snowball.

The police investigation had first reached the ears of the *Sun* at a time when Supt Clifton was still unsure what he was investigating. All he would say was that routine tests had discovered 'excess amounts' of insulin in the bloodstream of an unnamed boy, but it could mean anything, perhaps just a medical muddle or a clinical condition.

The Lincolnshire force issued a statement saying there was a 'possibility of discrepancies in the use of some prescribed drugs within the hospital'. It was still a 'sensitive enquiry in its early stages'. Hospital manager Mr Gibson revealed that he had called in the police as a 'precaution to look into a possible misuse'.

As the days ticked by, Supt Clifton continued to

describe the deaths at the hospital as 'unnatural but not necessarily malicious'.

He explained: 'From the outset of the enquiry we have attempted to tread the difficult path of carrying out the investigation, keeping the parents aware of what we are doing and not causing unnecessary suffering. It is extremely technical in nature because of the medical aspects involved. These aspects require much interpretation by experts in different fields.'

The cautious statements reflected police uncertainty in the early stages when they were still interviewing nurses, doctors and experts.

But word began to spread like wildfire as Supt Clifton's team of detectives began knocking on doors, talking to families about the treatment of their children on the ward and asking questions about the nurses. The town began to buzz with rumours about the scale of the police enquiry. There was no holding back the gathering tide of speculation in the close-knit market town and, in mid-June, the *Sun* broke the story that a nurse, so far unnamed, had been interviewed over the deaths of four children on the ward and given extended leave from her job. She was later named in the newspaper as Nurse Beverley Allitt.

The media descended on Grantham en masse, realising for the first time the sensational implications of the case. It was the first time that a nurse had been suspected of a serial killing in a British hospital.

The Angel and Royal was packed with journalists, radio reporters and photographers; TV camera crews lined up one after another outside the hospital to film the scene. Supt Clifton tried to stem the tide by telling reporters: 'We won't know if there is anything sinister until we meet the experts.'

At the hospital, administrator Mr Gibson was worried about the effects of the growing publicity, conscious that it could damage the confidence of his patients. He announced that a thorough review of internal security at the hospital, nursing systems and procedures had been carried out. He issued a statement in which he said the enquiry showed that they were 'all in order' and gave an assurance that there had been no further cause for alarm since the start of the police enquiry.

Most of the parents whose children had suffered on Ward Four were unaware of the real suspicion behind the police investigation.

Claire Peck's parents, David and Sue, learned more about the police enquiry from the pages of the *Sun*.

Sue had flown off on holiday with her parents to Yugoslavia, and husband David had stayed behind to start a new job, happy that his wife could make the trip. The change of scenery would do her good and perhaps help heal the wounds. Two months had passed since Claire had died from asthma, and Sue needed a break.

David, alone at home, read his morning newspaper which revealed that the police were investigating four deaths of children at the hospital. But there were no names of the dead children and he thought nothing of it. He didn't even save the report to show Sue when she returned.

But friends who met her at the airport, when she flew home five days later, told her about the revelations in the newspaper as they drove her home. Sue recalls: 'It just clicked with me and my parents straight away that it involved Claire. I had always suspected right from the day Claire died that something wasn't right. David had accepted the cause of her death was asthma but I couldn't forget Dr Porter saying to us: "Claire should never have died."

'When an experienced doctor tells you that, then you know something is very wrong.'

They decided to call the police the next day to ask if Claire was involved in the investigation.

They were asked to visit the police station; this wasn't something that could be talked about over the phone. They drove the fifteen miles down the A1 to Grantham wondering, but also fearing, what they were going to be told. It came as no surprise to be told that Claire's death was one of the four under investigation. Her death had been so unexpected, the detective told them, that it had to be examined. The police said they were treating it as suspicious.

Three days later, on 27 June, the day of Sue's twenty-sixth birthday, the police rang from Grantham with the news they had dreaded. The police officer said they were now sure that the post-mortem result had been wrong, that Claire hadn't died from asthma or other natural causes. They had blood samples and test results to prove it.

Her baffled parents wanted to know what, then, had killed her? David and Sue, in a state of shock, were told that their daughter had been given a 'fatal injection'. Sue didn't have to be told which of the nurses was being questioned by the police. 'I didn't need to be told it was Beverley Allitt. When I read the piece in the *Sun* it was her face that sprang into my mind. I knew it wouldn't be any of the other nurses.'

Sue's emotions were in turmoil. She had gone on holiday half suspecting that she was pregnant and now she was almost certain that she was expecting again. They had decided to have another baby even before Claire had died, and losing her had made them all the more determined. Their doctor had warned, however, that the trauma of the tragedy might make it difficult for Sue to conceive.

The day after the police phone call, just a little over two months since Claire's death, Sue rang the chemist to find out the result of her pregnancy test and was told: 'It's positive.'

Sue said: 'Claire had been our first child and had been very, very special to us. We felt we had been deprived of her lifetime but at least we had had her for fifteen months and we were grateful. Suddenly now we had something that gave us hope, to keep going and carry on.'

Still anxious to know what had killed their daughter, Sue and David went to the hospital where they were told that Claire had died from an overdose of potassium, detected in samples of blood taken on the night she died. They wanted to know why the samples had been taken. Did it mean that somebody had been suspicious about the reason for her relapse? They were stunned by the explanation.

Sue remembers: 'We were told that a doctor can tell when a child is going to die, but there had been no warning signs in Claire's case, that's why the blood had been taken. We realised that, if it hadn't been kept, there might have been nothing to test and nobody would have been any the wiser. Claire's death would have always been treated as natural.'

They made the decision soon afterwards that their new baby would not be born at Grantham and Kesteven Hospital. Sue said: 'The staff in the maternity ward had been wonderful when Claire was born but, after all we had been through, all we were being told about Claire's death, we knew we couldn't go back there. There were too many memories.'

Sue and David were delighted when a friend announced that he was organising a fund-raising dance to buy nebulisers for asthma sufferers. They threw themselves into the project, drawing comfort from the good that would come from Claire's tragic death.

In Grantham, and in the neighbouring towns and villages, other parents were hearing the same awful news about their children.

Timothy Hardwick's parents had read the story in the *Sun* with a sense of astonishment. By now three months had passed since Timothy's sudden, unexpected death on Ward Four. Robert and Helen Hardwick still found it hard to accept that their son was no more, but the coroner's officer had told them that he had died from cerebral palsy and epilepsy, and they had never once doubted the fact.

If they had harboured any suspicions, imagined for a minute that Timothy need not have died, then the news of the investigations at the hospital would have been easier for them to bear. As it was, the report that the police were enquiring into the deaths of four children and, worse still, the revelation that Nurse Allitt had been sent on extended leave, hit them like a bolt from the blue. For the first time Robert and Helen began to wonder whether their Timothy had died needlessly.

The couple decided to visit the social worker who had always taken such an interest in Timothy's welfare. He contacted the police at Grantham on their behalf and, within a couple of days, a sergeant and a policewoman were at their door.

Helen recalls: 'We didn't know what they would say when they came to the house. Up till then we had just accepted what we'd been told about Timothy's death but, when the officers came, they said right at the start that they weren't satisfied with the explanation that had appeared on the death certificate. They said Timothy's death was part of their enquiry. We'd always imagined that he'd been having an epileptic fit at the time he died, but they told us that hadn't been the case at all.'

In a state of bewilderment Robert and Helen waited for the police to return with more details. 'Eventually, when they came back, they near enough told us it was murder. They said they had found a very high level of potassium in Timothy's blood.'

Helen, whose Christian values had given her strength to face her own terrible handicap, wanted to know: 'How on earth can a person do such a wicked thing?' The policewoman, unable to provide the answer, could only tell Helen: 'We know how it happened, we know who did it, but we don't know why . . .'

Could it be, wondered Robert and Helen, that the killer thought death would be a blessing for the brain-damaged boy with the twinkling eyes. 'It was awful trying to understand why someone would want to harm our little boy,' said Helen. 'Someone who didn't know Timothy might think they were saving him from a lifetime of misery. But, in his own way, Timothy was happy, he wasn't suffering and he didn't deserve to die.'

The police were worried how Chris and Joanne Taylor would react to the news that baby Liam might have been murdered. Two police officers visited Joanne's best friend to ask how the couple were coping. The officers said they suspected 'something had gone wrong at the hospital', but told the friend not to tell Joanne or Chris about their suspicions. A week passed before the friend burst into tears and blurted out her secret to Joanne.

Joanne recalled: 'I was shaking with emotion. I couldn't take it in at first. I didn't want to believe it. Then I thought back to what Dr Nanayakkara had said when Liam died. He told us he was 99 per cent sure there was no medical explanation for his death. I felt so angry.'

The news hit Creswen O'Brien and her common-law husband, Mick Peasgood, hard. Their baby son Christopher had nearly died on Ward Four, but had now recovered. But they were still haunted by the cot death of their ten-month-old daughter, Michelle, two years earlier.

The first news of the investigation came in a telephone call from a Professor, three weeks after Christopher was discharged from hospital. He told the couple to expect a call from the police, but they couldn't wait.

'We rang the police at Grantham and asked about the enquiry, but they couldn't tell us anything. We heard nothing more until the next-door neighbour came round and told us it was on TV. The report said they were investigating the deaths of some children. I was furious. I went to the phone box and rang the police and asked them what the hell they were playing at.

'It was on TV and they had not had the decency to come and tell us.'

But when the police arrived two days later they said that Christopher's case was still being investi-

Angel of Death

gated; they were not sure whether or not he was
one of the children affected. Weeks later the police
returned with the news that they believed
Christopher's illness was suspicious.

Hazel and Robert Elstone returned home from
hospital in Nottingham to find two policewomen
on their doorstep. They said they wanted a statement about what had happened to their seven-
week-old baby son Patrick on Ward Four where
his heart had stopped beating twice.

The couple were baffled by the request until the
two officers broke the news that they were investigating the 'misuse of drugs'.

Hazel recalls: 'They asked if Patrick was diabetic.
I said he wasn't, but I thought it was strange they
should ask me that. It never crossed my mind that
anyone had tried to kill him. It's the last thing you
expect.

'He was in the safest place you could ever put a
baby – in hospital. I told the police that Patrick had
been having fits, and they said if he'd been given
insulin then that might explain it. But I still cannot
believe how anyone could harm little children. I
asked the police time and time again, but they
couldn't tell me.'

One by one other parents found the police at
their door asking questions, wanting to know what
they remembered about the treatment of their
children on Ward Four. At first the detectives
would only tell the families they were investigating
the wrongful use of drugs. There was no talk of
babies being poisoned, never mind murdered, and

190

not the merest hint that a nurse was the prime suspect.

The police had been uncertain how the parents would react to the news that the care of their children was under scrutiny. Detectives half expected to hear one or two complaints, grumbles about this and that but, instead, almost all the families stood fair square in defence of the hospital and its staff. The overwhelming response was that the children had been well cared for on the ward.

Only one couple, David and Kath Crampton, whose baby son Paul had suffered mysterious hypoglycemic attacks on the ward, had seriously challenged the belief that all was well. The results of the medical tests were proving their suspicions to be well founded.

14. 'Thank You Very Much'

Five months after the start of the police investigation, Sister Jean Saville found it all too much to bear.

The dawning realisation of the enormity of what had happened on Ward Four hit many of the nurses hard. They were gentle, caring people who had devoted their lives to helping sick people get better. Some were so badly distressed that they had been receiving counselling. All of them had been questioned by detectives, many of them several times, in the never-ending search for the slightest clue.

But on Friday, 20 September, two weeks after a police file accusing Beverley Allitt had been sent to the Director of Public Prosecutions, Sister Saville committed suicide.

She was the hospital's night services manager and one of the most senior nurses and respected members of staff. She had been on duty when a number of the youngsters had suffered unexplained heart attacks and respiratory failures, and she had helped in the battles to save young lives on Ward Four. She had helped save twin Katie Phillips and she had shared the anguish of Chris and Joanne Taylor on the night baby Liam had collapsed. She was forty-nine years old, a highly experienced and devoted nurse. She and her husband Barry had recently been on a holiday to Australia to celebrate their Silver Wedding anniversary.

The police interviews at the hospital had gone on for weeks and everybody was well aware by then that the detectives were investigating serious matters. What had happened to so many youngsters right under their noses? It was almost impossible for some nurses and doctors to accept that children had been murdered and that the finger of suspicion was pointing at a colleague they had trusted. For some, their very faith in human nature was being destroyed day by day.

But then, as the police enquiry was drawing to a close, Sister Saville took a massive overdose of Paracetamol at her home in the village of Leasingham, near Sleaford, and killed herself. There had been no warning of what was to happen. Jean Saville had told her farmer husband about the police investigation and her dislike of the questions. But she had always enjoyed her work and he didn't think she was worrying unduly about the events at the hospital.

But Sister Saville left a suicide note in which she wrote that she had nothing to do with the deaths of the children. She said: 'Please, please believe me.' There had never been any suggestion that she had been involved in the deaths of the children.

Like many of the nurses she hadn't wanted to be interviewed by the police, but she'd faced their questions, answered them honestly and had never been a suspect. Nobody fully realised the effect the investigation was having on the kindly and popular nurse.

On the morning of her death Barry left for work but, when he arrived home at 7.45pm, he found a 100-tablet box lying empty and his wife dead in their bed in her nightdress. Her body was taken, ironically, to the Grantham and Kesteven Hospital, where she had spent so many years of her life, and placed in the mortuary to await a post-mortem examination.

Relatives were in no doubt what had driven Jean to take her own life. Her father-in-law, Ernest Saville, who lived just a few doors away, said: 'Jean left a note saying she definitely had nothing to do with the deaths. I think it just got too much for her. She was so upset that the babies were dying on the ward where she was in charge. I believe that hospital affair just upset her so much she couldn't take it. She was perfectly happy otherwise.'

Several of the families who had seen their children survive on the ward, thanks to her skill, attended the funeral, determined to pay their final respects to a nurse whose devotion to saving lives had been legendary in Grantham. Sue and Peter Phillips were among those who would remain eternally grateful to Sister Saville. She had been the nurse who had refused to give in, battled against the odds and won, the night their baby Katie nearly died on the Children's Ward. They knew they had her to thank for Katie's life.

Sue Phillips recalls: 'It had certainly got to Jean. When we spoke to her about it, Bev had already been given extended leave from the hospital. Jean told us she just couldn't understand how things had happened to the children. Everything was taking place on her ward and it was really upsetting her. She was disgusted.

'Somehow she felt responsible and felt she should have been able to do something to stop it. She was such a caring person. She'd lived for nursing, she'd done so much to help people. When we heard she was dead, it was just awful.

'There were really five deaths on Ward Four – the children plus Jean Saville.'

Her suicide raised obvious questions about whether she had ever come under suspicion herself. At the inquest into her death the coroner took the unusual step of clearing her name. Deputy Sleaford coroner, Glyn Williams, refused to read aloud her handwritten note which had made it clear she had intended to take her own life. But he announced: 'I have made enquiries, and I have spoken to the police, and they are satisfied that she had no involvement in the tragic deaths which have recently occurred at Grantham hospital.'

Other nurses, too, had been finding it hard to carry on their duties. The strain became so acute that the Royal College of Nursing offered its members counselling to help them cope. Hospital manager Martin Gibson announced that a consultant had visited the hospital and agreed there was a need for a trained and sympathetic person to consider 'all aspects of the effects staff are feeling from the current situation'.

While the pressure grew amongst her former colleagues, Allitt remained on 'extended leave'. But her 'holiday' was interrupted when she was summoned to return to Grantham police station for more questioning.

This time the police directly accused her, for the first time, of murdering the four children and attempting to kill the others.

Instead of repeating her protests of innocence, Allitt remained tight-lipped, exercising her right to remain silent, refusing to answer one question. A detective said: 'We had prepared all our questions but, as we went through each case, Allitt just stared ahead and said nothing. At the most she would say: "No comment."

We put it to her quite forcibly that she had murdered the children but she didn't say anything. She didn't even tell us that she hadn't done it. All the interview was taped but there was nothing to listen to except our own voices.' She was eventually allowed to leave the police station with her bail extended.

Supt Clifton's file on the case, 118 pages long and more complex than anything he had ever prepared in twenty-five years as a policeman, was being slowly assessed by the Director of Public Prosecutions in London. It would be up to him to decide whether the detectives had managed to amass enough evidence to bring any charges.

Supt Clifton suggested there should be twelve charges in all, four accusing Allitt of murdering Liam Taylor, Timothy Hardwick, Becky Phillips and Claire Peck, and another eight offences alleging the attempted murder of Kayley Desmond, Paul Crampton, Bradley Gibson, Henry Chan, Katie Phillips, Christopher Peasgood, Christopher King and Patrick Elstone. The evidence was amassed and all he could do now was sit back and await a decision.

Parents whose children had suffered at the hospital were anxious to know just how long it would take. Their lives had been ripped apart by the enquiry and now, after five months, they thought they had waited long enough for some answers. A police spokesman predicted there would be news in five weeks or so and, when there was no word by mid October, the families ran out of patience, complaining that 'red tape' had ground the enquiry to a halt.

They had formed their own Support Group, united by the knowledge that they all had children who had died or had survived the incidents on Ward Four. It gave them a chance to share their grief with others and to talk about their problems in a process that would help each one of them to come to terms with what had happened. Their leader was Mrs Judith Gibson whose five-year-old son, Bradley, was one of the survivors.

The strain of not knowing whether charges would be brought, and the fear that the case would be buried for lack of evidence, was beginning to tell. The families decided to call a press conference at Grantham Guildhall to voice their growing concern. About twenty journalists from national and local newspapers, TV and radio stations scribbled furiously as first one parent, then another, revealed their emotions. Seven families appeared before the cameras, along with a Manchester-based solicitor, Ann Alexander, who had offered to help them bring a civil action against the hospital because of their suffering and the possibility of long-term effects on their children.

Several of the surviving youngsters had shown worrying signs of possible brain damage after their ordeal at the hospital; nobody would know for sure until the children were much older. Tests were being carried out on Katie Phillips who developed an apparent weakness on her right side; Hazel Elstone had noticed that surviving son Patrick wasn't making the same progress as his twin brother, Anthony; and Finbar and Margaret Desmond were unhappy about the development of daughter Kayley. Others believed their children may have escaped without long-term effects. The lawyer immediately launched a claim for damages on behalf of several of the children.

If the police enquiry fizzled out, and the case was dropped, then the parents announced they would consider bringing their own private prosecution.

The press conference was a traumatic experience for most of the families, exposed to the glare of publicity for the very first time, but they were determined to have their say.

Chris Taylor, whose seven-week-old baby son Liam had been the first to die, sat beside his wife Joanne in the upstairs conference room at the Guildhall and criticised the hospital authorities. He snapped: 'They have referred to the strain their staff have been under, but I've not heard them once mention the strain the parents are under.' He continued: 'If our three-year-old son became ill now, then I wouldn't take him to the hospital. I don't feel I can trust anyone until we get some answers.

'We were just trying to come to terms with what we had lost when the police came. We'd no suspicions before that and we still haven't had the answer why he died . . .'

Judith Gibson, whose son Bradley had suffered two unexplained heart attacks on the ward, and 'died' for thirty-two minutes, said the case had put a strain on marriages. She spoke of the need for a quick decision from the DPP, saying: 'None of us want to go through this any longer. We have all suffered enough. We are all experiencing very similar emotions and feelings. We feel someone is culpable, and that someone is responsible at the hospital for the deaths of these four children. The families want that person found and prosecuted.'

Sue Phillips was in no doubt there should be a public enquiry, compensation for the parents and a speedy decision from the DPP.

She told the newsmen: 'As parents we are trying to stick together, and see it through together, but it still hasn't sunk in what's happened, and it won't for a long time. It's like a nightmare. I keep thinking I'll wake up. The police have told us what was administered to our baby Becky, and exactly how much. In some ways I feel very sorry for the person who did this to her. The person must be twisted.'

Strangely, throughout the hour-long press conference, nobody mentioned Beverley Allitt's name. It wasn't necessary. Everyone in the room knew who had brought them all together and who was the real target of their fury. Finbar Desmond, whose daughter Kayley had been nine months old when she twice suffered respiratory failures on Ward Four, said he knew the nurse who had been questioned by the police.

'I feel compassion for her,' he said. 'I've not seen her since all this blew up, but I don't think I'd like to meet her because I don't know how I would react . . .'

Lawyer Ms Alexander did her best, measuring her words carefully to explain what the parents thought, knowing that there was no way, in the middle of a murder enquiry, that she could name the suspected killer.

She said: 'They believe one person is responsible, and they think they know who that person is. The parents are under a lot of stress because they don't know whether the police will be allowed to bring a criminal prosecution. That is hanging over them.'

She said the delay in deciding whether to bring charges was causing undue distress. Parents were not unhappy, she said, with the police who had kept them in the picture 'every inch of the way'. But turning to the role of the hospital authorities in the tragedy, and the apparent delay in calling in the police at the beginning, she declared: 'The parents haven't had any questions answered as to the reason why there was a delay in bringing in the police in the first place.

'The incidents started in February, but it wasn't until May that the police were involved. They are concerned that not only does it not happen again, but also that steps are taken to ensure that it does not.'

The idea of the press conference had been to arouse public feeling and to put into words the suspicion that the deaths on Ward Four might be swept under the carpet. To that extent it was a huge success.

Lincolnshire's Assistant Chief Constable, Alan Goldsmith, quickly issued a statement sympathising with the parents. 'We understand what they are going through,' he said. 'But the file has been with the DPP for four weeks and is still being considered very thoroughly.'

Hospital manager Martin Gibson, worried by the criticism that he had been slow to react, jumped to the hospital's defence and insisted that he had called in the police as soon as the possibility of drugs being misused had been identified. Security on the wards had been checked. 'Both ourselves and the police are satisfied as to their adequacy,' he said.

Mr Gibson said it was the first time the hospital had heard about a call for a public enquiry; he felt parents should contact him if they were anxious about the treatment of their children on Ward Four. Any claims for compensation would be carefully considered, he promised.

The press conference generated a huge wave of publicity, making headlines in almost all the national newspapers and on TV.

Parents, however, still harboured doubts that the enquiry would not lead to charges and that the case would be too complicated to prove.

On 13 November, when they had still heard nothing (almost two months after the file had gone to the DPP), their patience ran out again. After a meeting with their lawyer, a group resorted to shock tactics, besieging Grantham police station and demanding to know why there was still no news. The angry parents crowded into the foyer of the station before they were finally summoned into an office for a meeting with Detective Chief Inspector Alan Smith.

Judith Gibson stormed: 'The waiting is driving us mad. We have to be told what's happening.' Joining in the verbal attack Chris Taylor said: 'We've had to take action to break down the wall of silence which surrounds the case. We've read more in the press than the police have been prepared to tell us.'

The parents finally left the station an hour later, feeling reassured. The Detective Chief Inspector had promised frequent progress reports, and said:

'Even if there is nothing to report the parents will be told.'

Mrs Gibson told reporters: 'We made our point, and the police appreciated that. I am sure we shall now see some light.'

They only had to wait eight more days.

Supt Clifton had arranged to meet officials of the DPP and medical experts in Nottingham on 20 November to discuss the next move; a decision would then be taken whether or not to charge Nurse Allitt.

The meeting was scheduled to last two days but they didn't need that long. By the afternoon of the first day everybody agreed there was only one course of action to take.

Supt Clifton, who had had that gut feeling from the beginning, and who had refused to walk away when the investigation had seemed hopeless, was told: 'You can charge her.' Allitt could be charged with the murder of all four children. He could also charge her with attempting to kill the eight who had survived, and also assaulting them, causing grievous bodily harm with intent.

He decided not to waste a minute; he had waited a long time for this day, and so had the families of the twelve children.

Allitt, on police bail since her first visit to Grantham police station, had spent what was to be her last day of freedom answering the phone, relaying messages and packing Christmas hampers at the wine warehouse where her father worked at Corby Glen.

Managing director, Jeremy Marshall-Roberts, knew about the allegations and had even had the police at his door asking questions. During the weeks of speculation he had asked Allitt about the case, and been told: 'I didn't do it . . .' But Mr Marshall-Roberts knew that Allitt realised that, even if she could prove her innocence, she would never be allowed to nurse children again. In his mind Jeremy Marshall-Roberts felt the police had made an awful mistake.

Allitt was at home 250 yards away when her solicitor, Mr John Kendall, broke the news. Mr Kendall was a well-known figure in Grantham, an articulate man with a ready smile and a firm hand-shake.

He was no stranger to Stuart Clifton. The two men had known each other for five years, opposing one another across the courtrooms of Lincolnshire. In one murder case, handled by Supt Clifton, Kendall had defended a man accused of battering his father to death – and had won the day. On other occasions he had lost, but there was no animosity between the two professionals, simply mutual respect.

Now he found himself on opposite sides again to the detective superintendent. He had already amassed a huge file of information about the events on Ward Four, and had even gone so far as to advise his client to read *The Death Shift*, the book telling the story of Nurse Genene Jones's conviction for murdering a child. There were similarities between the two cases, and Mr

Kendall had been conscious that Allitt should study the book.

He had known that the conference on that November Wednesday was likely to produce a decision, but he had expected that it would be days, or even weeks, before he heard the outcome. However, by 8pm of that same night, Supt Clifton was on the phone to his home asking if he would deliver Allitt to the police station to be charged.

Supt Clifton and colleague Detective Inspector Neil Jones went to Grantham to await her arrival.

News of the impending charges came as a heart-rending blow to her family. The realisation of what was to come began to sink in as Allitt prepared to leave for the police station. She could take no personal possessions with her, no change of clothes, no favourite book or tape. Mr Kendall knew from experience that it was better if Allitt 'went into the system clean'.

It was Neil Jones, the officer who had tracked down the children's blood samples, who was given the job of charging her.

Detectives who had spent more than six months investigating the events on Ward Four thought that now Allitt would betray some emotion, perhaps shed a tear or scream in frustration.

But she showed no concern as Mr Jones read out the charges, one by one. With solicitor Mr Kendall at her side Allitt, by then just twenty-three, listened in silence, saying nothing, as he listed each one of the four charges of murder – eight-week-old Liam Taylor, eleven-year-old Timothy Hardwick, nine-week-old Becky Phillips, fifteen-month-old Claire Peck.

Then came eight charges of attempting to murder and eight more of assault causing grievous bodily harm to Katie Phillips, Henry Chan, Kayley Desmond, Patrick Elstone, Christoper Peasgood, Christopher King, Bradley Gibson and Paul Crampton.

As he finished Allitt finally spoke. She said simply: 'Thank you very much.' One officer recalled: 'We couldn't believe it. We talked about it afterwards. There she was being charged with the murders of four children and the attempted murder of another eight and all she could say was "Thank you very much." She treated it like a Sunday school outing.'

He added: 'The surprising thing we noticed was the difference in her attitude, depending whether it was a conversation or an interview. In conversation she was very comfortable, very personable, but the minute you got into an interview situation it was as though someone had thrown a switch. It was like talking to two different personalities.'

Allitt was taken back to the row of police cells where she had spent her first night during questioning back in June, to await her first appearance in Grantham Magistrates' Court the following morning.

After all their months of anxious waiting Supt Clifton wanted to ensure that the parents were the first to know about the charges.

A detective telephoned David Crampton, who had been designated to take the first call. David, an intelligent, professional man, had worked closely with Supt Clifton and was in no doubt about his ability to discover the truth. 'If I had committed a crime and knew Stuart Clifton was after me, then I'd give myself up,' he said. He let the other families know the news. Some were quietly delighted but Peter Phillips couldn't hide his excitement and decided to go straight to Ward Four, where Katie was still under observation, to break the news to the other nurses.

He said: 'I walked in, punching the air, shouting to the nurses that she had been charged. I expected them to be pleased that the waiting was finally over but virtually all of them walked away.' This was not a night for celebration on Ward Four.

Knowing that she had been accused of murdering four children, the police doubted whether Allitt would get much sleep. Innocent or guilty, how could anyone rest with that hanging over her? But the next morning the young nurse was so soundly asleep that she had to be woken up to face the magistrates.

'We all found it totally amazing,' remembered one of the detectives. 'You'd think that if you faced all those charges, you wouldn't sleep a wink.'

News of Allitt's impending appearance before the magistrates bench had caused angry crowds to gather outside Grantham Court. Among them were Peter and Sue Phillips, Robert and Hazel Elstone, Finbar Desmond, and Judith and Stephen Gibson, all of whom had endured days and nights of heartbreak on Ward Four.

The police wondered if Allitt's composure would crumble as they prepared to escort her to the courtroom in a van with its windows meshed for extra security. One officer said. 'She didn't ask for a blanket to cover her face. It was as if she was relishing the attention she was getting. If you hadn't known better you'd have thought she didn't realise the implications of what was happening.'

Only when Allitt came within sight of the Court, saw the crowds who had waited three hours to catch sight of her, and heard the barrage of abuse and the jeers, did she react.

She asked one of the officers: 'Are they going to hurt me?'

The police, concerned for the safety of their prisoner, threw a jacket over Allitt's head as the van pulled to a halt outside the Court. She was led upstairs into courtroom Number One at 11.58am, wearing a grey jumper, purple T-shirt, black jeans and trainers.

It had taken 204 days from the first day of the investigation to put Allitt into court.

Now there were fifty people trying to pack into the first-floor courtroom to see her. Every seat was filled and parents and relatives were allowed to stand, lining the green-painted walls, as Allitt was brought in to stand impassively in front of the three duty magistrates.

Parents were so close they could have reached out to touch her, but nobody tried. After the noisy, angry scenes outside, the silence was over-whelming as prosecuting solicitor, Philip Howes, rose to ask for Allitt to be remanded in custody for her own safety.

He told bench chairman, Mr Norman Dodson: 'Feeling is running high in the locality, especially as far as the parents are concerned. There is a clear risk to this woman's safety if you grant bail. Although she has been on bail, charges have now been brought and she realises the enormity of what she faces.'

Mr Kendall was keen to try to calm the rising tide of feeling, and asked for the normal reporting restrictions to be lifted so that the press could publish his announcement that Allitt would be pleading not guilty to all the allegations. He added: 'The charges will be fought at the appropriate time and place.'

The hearing lasted just four minutes and Allitt was remanded in custody in New Hall Women's Prison, near Wakefield, Yorkshire.

A photograph of Nurse Allitt's face appeared on the front page of almost every newspaper in Britain. The picture, taken in a happier moment, showed her cradling tiny baby, twin Katie Phillips, in her arms.

But there was to be no way now she could ever expect to become Katie's godmother.

Also blazed across the newspapers and on TV bulletins were vivid pictures of Liam Taylor's grandmother, Shirley Little.

She was not a woman to forgive and forget.

As Allitt was driven away to prison, Shirley could contain her fury no longer and was pictured waving her fists and lunging at the police van, shouting: 'Remember me, you bleeder.'

She had seen her grandson die in agonising circumstances and had then had to return to the hospital where she worked as a ward orderly.

Liam's mother, Joanne, said: 'We were all furious when we realised what had happened to Liam. My mother wanted to see her face to face. She even used to pedal up to Allitt's house on her pushbike, just in case she could catch sight of her.'

Shirley took her revenge on Allitt by sticking pins in a photograph snipped from a newspaper; she kept this secretly hidden under a cushion on her settee. Joanne said: 'I found it one day and screwed it up, thinking it was just a piece of old newspaper. My mum complained because she said she had not finished with it.'

On the morning after Allitt's first appearance, Joanne took a taxi to her mother's house. The driver was full of sympathy for the nurse whose photograph appeared on every front page. He half turned to Joanne, not realising that her baby was among those who had died, and said: 'Isn't it a shame – they have found her guilty before it's proved.'

Joanne said: 'I just flew at him. I found myself screaming at him, I was so angry. I just went on and on at the poor bloke who didn't realise at first what he had said that was wrong. He was in a real state. When he drove off he was all flustered.'

Joanne and husband Chris had both found them-selves drawn to the house where Allitt had been living in Grantham. Before she was arrested they would both drive there, wind down the window and stare at the front door in the hope of catching sight of the suspended nurse. Joanne said: 'The funny thing was whenever I saw the house, my mind went numb and my legs would wobble and go to jelly.'

She had come face to face with Allitt just once since the day Liam had died on Ward Four. Two weeks after his death, friends had taken her into town for a night out to help her get over the tragedy and she spotted Allitt relaxing with her pals in the King's Arms. Joanne was still grateful for the kindness Allitt had shown – still unaware of what was to come.

Joanne said: 'All I wanted to do was go and talk to her about Liam. I told my friends that I was going to say thank you to her for looking after Liam. Allitt was with six or seven friends, and I tapped her on the arm. I was all choked up. I remember saying: "I want to thank you for looking after Liam."

'She just nodded her head and didn't say anything. I couldn't say any more, because I was so upset. I thought she would have shown some feelings but there was nothing there. It was almost as though we had never met.'

She went on: 'Now I don't feel any pity for her, only hatred. There are nights when I lie in bed and I can picture her standing and looking at Liam. What I would like more than anything is the chance to sit down and talk to her.

'I want to know why she chose Liam. She was with him for nineteen hours in total. She must have known what he was going through all the time. She was supposed to be caring for him.'

Chris said: 'Myra Hindley killed children but she was not in a position of trust, working with them in hospital. If you can't trust a nurse, then who can you trust?'

15. 'Close the Ward'

News of the murder charges failed to sway the view of Allitt's family that the police were making an awful mistake. Most of the villagers in Corby Glen stayed loyal, refusing to believe that she was capable of the killings.

But friend Tracy Jobson began to doubt this view. As she waited for the trial she became convinced that her friend was a killer of babies.

She said: 'I decided that one charge can be a mistake, but when there are twelve then commonsense tells you . . . Everyone who knows Bev still can't believe she did it. I can't believe it, but I know she has. It's possible someone could do it if they're a bit weird, something out of the ordinary. If you try and compare it with a multi-murderer like the Ripper, Peter Sutcliffe – he had some sort of reason, didn't he? He didn't like prostitutes, but there's no reason behind what's happened here.

'Maybe she didn't like babies, but what reason is that? You can think that maybe something was telling her that she couldn't let little babies live, but what's the reason?'

It was the absence of a motive that bewildered Tracy. None of the children had been grievously ill when they had been admitted to hospital, and the senselessness of it all appalled her. Also, like many other nurses, she feared the case could have a long-term effect on the hospital. How many parents, she wondered, would think twice about leaving their children in hospital in future?

If her friend had really murdered Liam Taylor, Timothy Hardwick, Becky Phillips and Claire Peck, there was one question Tracy needed answering: 'How can you murder a baby at work and then carry on absolutely normally?'

Her mother, who had listened to Allitt's denials and believed them for so long, could understand how so many people had been fooled. But even she wondered how, if she really was the killer on Ward Four, she could have done it and yet remain the same girl?

She said: 'There are a lot of people at the hospital feel a lot of guilt. They feel they should have seen things and should have known but, really, there was no way of knowing what was going on. When you look back you think: "God!" '

If her friend was really a monster, Tracy accepted that her crimes would find a place in history. 'What you've got is the biggest serial murderer in a British hospital ever – the strangest, weirdest murderer there has ever been. But you'll never get a true insight into who she was, or what she was really like, unless you knew her . . .'

Mrs Jobson, her voice shaking with anger, declared: 'I wish to God I could shut my eyes and pretend it never happened. The trouble is that the more you knew Beverley Allitt, the more normal she appeared in every way. Absolutely. I'll never understand her as long as I live.

'I think she's very sick. But, at the same time, I think she knew what she was doing. She's calculating but I think she can't help herself. She can manipulate people, but she doesn't come over as a forceful character.

'You tend to feel sorry for her. That's how she got you to think, she wanted you to feel sorry for her. I felt sorry for her when she first came here to my house. She went into hospital twice while she was here.

'I don't think anyone is going to get any answers, even after the trial. I would love to have it all explained to me, why this and why that, but I don't think anyone is going to get answers and explanations.

'I don't think there's anything in her past that you could say this caused it, or that caused it. It's not like she came from a broken home, or she'd been beaten or her parents were divorced. It's very strange.

'The weird things that were happening here were her just looking for attention, but she was getting all the attention anyway. At the same time I was keeping the press away from her; I was looking after her. I treated her like another daughter.

'I am writing my story about what happened here. Even if it comes out two years after the trial, people will still want to read it, they really will. I don't think anybody can imagine what I went through while Beverley was in my house. People will read it and say: "That's unbelievable." Nobody will believe it. But I'm doing it for my benefit. It's almost a therapy.

'I am feeling the reaction. I know a lot of people have been touched by what happened, especially those who have lost children, but it's bad, too, for those whose children could have died. I don't think anybody realises that. There's more than one way of being damaged.

'I feel as though I have been in a state of shock for six or seven months and, to be honest, I still am. The same with Jonathan. It changes your view on people. It makes you question your own judgement.

'I know I am not the only one she took in. Nobody could have foreseen it either. I don't think it could have happened in any other way than it did. At the hospital the administrators and the doctors were all taken in, they were all victims.

'I know some people are complaining that it went on for as long as it did before it was stopped, but the truth is that I am sure if it had been happening on a geriatric ward, it could have still been going on and nobody would have known.

'You don't notice it when old folk die. They are expected to die suddenly. Babies aren't, are they?'

As Beverley Allitt was taken away from Grantham Magistrates' Court, on her way to a cell at Wakefield, the anger of the parents turned on the hospital.

There were demands for a public enquiry into how so many children had been struck down before the police were called in. And there were questions about how Allitt had been allowed to become a nurse.

But it was a wordy statement issued by Mr Martin Gibson, on behalf of the Grantham and Kesteven Hospital, that first infuriated them. Couched in official language, his statement said:

1. The Authority has been co-operating closely with the Lincolnshire Police since calling them in at the end of April to investigate unexpected outcomes in treatment on the Children's Ward at Grantham and Kesteven General Hospital.

2. Having been informed by the police that a former member of staff, who worked on the Children's Ward at the time, has been charged with causing the death and mistreatment of a number of child patients, I would like to say how shocked and saddened the staff of the hospital are at this news, and to express our deepest and most heartfelt sympathy to the families of those children involved in this tragic episode.

   The families who live locally, of all the children whose treatment has at any time been the subject of the police investigations, were seen privately by senior hospital staff as soon as practicable after it became clear that the initial enquiries involved their child, except where the patients declined the offer of a visit (one other family was seen by a local social worker).

During these conversations the concern and
sympathy of all our staff for the families were
made clear. It was felt that a public or formal
expression of sympathy on the hospital's part
should not be made until it was clearer which
children were considered by the police to have
been involved.

That stage has now been reached, and a formal letter is going to the families involved, from
the Vice-Chairman of the Health Authority, in
the absence of the Chairman.

Our responses to specific media questions
about the effect of the events on the other staff
at the hospital have been represented by some
as showing a lack of concern for the families
and children involved. Nothing could be further
from the truth. We have provided, or ensured
that others provide, practical help to all the
families where it is needed.

For example, we have arranged for Lincolnshire Social Services to organise offers of long-
term care to all the families. In providing help,
we have been careful not to add needlessly to
the grief and worry of those whose children's
care and treatment were unaffected by these
events.

3. We confirm that the arrangements for hospital
security have been checked, and both the
hospital and the police are satisfied as to their
adequacy. There has been no further cause for
concern since the police were called in.

4. Parents of the children involved have been

seen, and in some cases continue to be seen, by the Health Authority's staff. If any parents have any anxieties about treatment of their child on the Children's Ward at the hospital in the months January to April of this year, they should contact the General Manager's Office at the hospital and arrangements will be made for them to be seen by medical or nursing staff.

5. As criminal proceedings have been started, the matter is sub judice and the authority can make no further comment until the proceedings have been concluded.

When parents gathered the following day at their regular meeting place in the King's Arms in the centre of Grantham, Mr Gibson's statement provoked outrage.

As far as some families were concerned the hospital had done nothing to help them in their hours and weeks of need. They hit back in a statement saying: 'At no time has Grantham Hospital taken any positive action to support the families during the period of the police investigation.'

Chris Taylor declared: 'The parents have received help from their GPs, health visitors and other specialists – but we have sought that treatment ourselves.'

Mr Gibson responded to the criticism, saying that, if the hospital had failed to provide practical help where it was needed, 'then we can only apologise, and do so unreservedly'.

The next day families received letters from the

South Lincolnshire Health Authority, expressing 'sincere and heartfelt condolences' and offering help if required. The Health Authority had asked the local council Social Services Department to coordinate support services for the families.

Peter and Sue Phillips issued another statement saying: 'We cannot find it in our hearts to blame the hospital or the staff for what has happened.' They were later to change their minds and announced that they would not use the Grantham Hospital again. At that stage they also called for an enquiry into how Allitt had been allowed to become a nurse, and why she was given the job of caring for sick babies on a one-to-one basis when she was so inexperienced.

They suggested that the Children's Ward should even be closed down and revamped before being reopened again with a complete new staff. 'Then,' declared Sue in a letter to Mr Gibson, 'you might start getting some credibility back – the credibility the hospital and the rest of the staff deserve.'

Sue Peck, whose daughter Claire had been the last to die, had always disliked Nurse Allitt from the moment she had deliberately snubbed her daughter on the Ward.

When she was finally told that Allitt had been charged, furious Sue snapped: 'I always thought it would be that bitch. We think it is absolutely disgusting. We now know that a baby had died in February, things had been happening throughout March and April, but the hospital didn't close down the Ward.

'We have heard that there were more than twenty incidents on the one ward. If we had known that so many children had died, or suffered cardiac arrests, we would not have taken Claire anywhere near the place. OK, they have charged Beverley Allitt, but we feel the hospital is, in some way, to blame. Why weren't the police called in until the week after Claire died?

'If the hospital had acted promptly, then Claire's death might have been avoided. We want a public enquiry to find out all these answers. In our mind, they allowed Beverley Allitt to get away with it for too long.

'I am determined she is not going to ruin the rest of our life. She's taken Claire and we will not be able to forget about that, but she's not going to ruin the rest of our life.

'I wish I could tell her that.

'I wish I knew why it had all happened.'

Husband David said: 'We feel that something should have been done a lot sooner by the hospital. Claire was the last of four children to die, and her death was the most preventable.'

Beverley Allitt was remanded in custody to await her next court appearance and trial.

But the police began to wonder if she would live long enough to stand trial. Allitt was given a cell to herself where everything was coloured green – the walls, the toilet, the washbasin, even a green-painted bed. She was kept apart from the other prisoners for her own protection, in the same way that child sex offenders are segregated.

She had been there less than a week when she fell, injuring her hand and wrist in the prison gymnasium. She was taken to the prison hospital where her wrist was heavily strapped; it was decided to keep her there instead of returning her to her cell.

The next day rumours reached Grantham that Allitt had taken a suspected overdose of Paracetamol. The prison governor told reporters that it wasn't true, that Allitt was being kept in the hospital for her own safety. 'When someone is facing charges like this, we do not want to take any chances. There is always the possibility they may try to take their own life,' he said. In Grantham, Allitt's solicitor, Mr Kendall, dismissed the rumour, insisting that 'it's simply not true'.

Friends and relatives remained convinced that Allitt was not the killer that the police alleged. In the village of Corby Glen, everyone seemed united in the view that Beverley, whom they had watched grow up among them, was innocent of the dreadful crimes she was accused of committing.

Her devoted parents, Lillian and Richard, remained loyal to their daughter, refusing to believe for one moment that she was capable of killing anyone, let alone four children at the hospital. They made the 180-mile round trip to visit her in prison every Saturday, bearing their own ordeal 'with remarkable fortitude'.

Allitt's grandmother, grey-haired pensioner Dorothy Burrows, who shared the family's conviction that Beverley was innocent, said: 'Richard and Lillian are suffering as much as the parents who have lost children. I cannot conceive she would ever harm a child, and Richard and Lillian feel the same way.

'Bev is a dedicated nurse; there's something wrong somewhere. I think the police have made a mistake. Bev has written to me from prison, and she keeps saying to me and to other people, that we haven't got to worry. She says they are good to her in prison and she's not on her own all the time. She's taken up embroidery. It hardly seems fair, locking Bev up when she has done nothing.

'Nobody can say whether it is true or not; we will have to wait for the outcome of the trial. We've never had anything like this in our family before, and in my mind Beverley's innocent.'

Allitt's closest childhood friend, Rachel Smith, will never forget seeing her face on the front page of every national newspaper. 'I'll always remember seeing her on TV, being led into court; then I went into the local shop and there was Bev's face on all the front pages. It was a horrible picture, it made her look really bad, and I really felt for Bev.

'When I saw some of our old schoolfriends later they knew I'd been closer to Bev than anyone, and they were asking me: "Did she do it?" "What did I think?" All I could say was that I didn't know.'

The police called twice, wanting to know if Rachel had ever doubted her friend's honesty, or could tell them anything that might help their case against Allitt. 'The police asked what Bev was like, but there's nothing I could say to criticise her. She was always a nice girl. It affected me deeply when she was in court. I didn't believe she'd done it, and I won't believe it until she's convicted, and even then I don't know whether I will.

'I'd just like to see Bev, sit down with her and talk about it. Her life has always revolved around kids. I could never imagine her harming them. To do that you'd have to have no feelings at all.'

The people of Corby Glen, who still trusted her as a friend and respected her parents, remained loyal in the face of everything. The village was a law-abiding community, a place where the locals knew right from wrong, but there was a feeling, nonetheless, that the police had got it hopelessly wrong. Allitt's parents, Richard and Lillian, were comforted by the support of their neighbours.

Jeremy Marshall-Roberts, managing director of the wine company where Allitt had worked on her last day of freedom, felt the police had given way to pressure from the parents of the children. He was in no doubt that a ghastly mistake had been made. 'Even now I'd happily let Bev come and babysit at our house, and quite a few families feel that way in Corby Glen.'

The Rector of Corby Glen, the Rev. Ron Amis, had only moved to the village a few weeks earlier, but he was impressed by the loyalty of his parishioners. There was no backbiting or nastiness; instead, there was a common desire to protect her family.

He'd seen the anguish of Allitt's parents for himself. They were good people, but the burden and the worry had devastated their life. 'They are trying to cope, trying to keep going, but if you want to see what brokenness is then it's there with them.'

As for the allegations, the Rector knew where the village stood. 'If you went door to door you'd get the same reaction from people – they don't believe it's true.'

Steve Biggs, who had been the only real love of Allitt's life, found it impossible to comprehend. The police had questioned him several times, told him about the unexpected deaths at the hospital and shared their suspicions, but he'd still been shocked when he heard that his former fiancée had been charged with killing the children.

'The police told me they thought Bev had been copying a nurse in America who'd been convicted of killing a child. They also said she may have been suffering from Munchausen Syndrome. That's possible because Bev always loved to be the centre of attention, but even so I was stunned by the news that she'd been accused.

'I've seen the violent side of Bev's nature, very few people have ever seen that, but even I don't think she's capable of doing something as awful as this. She treated me badly, but I can't think she would go and kill four children. I don't know whether it's because I still feel a little bit for Bev, but it just doesn't make sense.'

At Pauline's grocery store, where Allitt had worked part-time as a girl, Pauline herself was sure it was all a mistake. The police had been to see her, like many people in the village, 'but there's nobody who'll say a bad word about Bev here.'

Dawn Greetham, who had been in the Girl Guides with Allitt and been proud to be her pal at school, was at the factory where she worked as a machinist when BBC Radio One broadcast news of the nurse's appearance in court.

'One of my workmates heard Bev's name, and honestly I couldn't believe it. People who know Bev can't imagine she would ever do something like this.'

Amid the trauma there were, just occasionally, moments of amusement. Allitt loved bananas but the prison had banned them, seeming to take the view that they were almost as much of a threat as keys and files in cakes. They decided that prisoners could make mind-blowing booze out of the skins which contained high levels of potassium. Mr Kendall did his best to help and, whenever she left the gaol for routine remand hearings, he made sure there was a bunch of her favourite fruit on hand.

The court hearings were emotional events for the parents who found themselves drawn to the court, desperate not to miss the sight of Allitt in handcuffs. She was a focus of their hatred. It was almost as if seeing her would help them understand what had happened.

But there was no look of remorse on Allitt's face, no sign that she was sorry for what had happened to their children, even if she was innocent of the charges. Instead she smiled openly each time she arrived at court, enraging the watching families.

Creswen O'Brien, whose baby son Christopher had been among the survivors, couldn't control her anger and ran at the police van, screaming at Allitt: 'How can you come to court with a bleeding smile on your face? You tried to kill my son.' Creswen became so furious that she added a few expletives right in front of the watching policemen and she was warned to behave herself.

By the time of Allitt's next appearance, Creswen had already decided that she was guilty. 'There are times when the anger inside us is almost unbearable and those are the times you'd like to be able to get at her.'

Solicitor Mr Kendall felt Allitt smiled 'out of nervousness', but understood how it upset the parents. It had been suggested she should go to court covered by a blanket, but Kendall said: 'Beverley says she is not guilty, and she has got nothing to hide.'

The parents reacted in different ways, many deciding that, in their minds, Allitt was already guilty, even though she still had not been committed for trial by the magistrates.

Chris Taylor, whose son Liam had been the first to die, had even driven to Allitt's home on several occasions before she had been charged. He said: 'What I would have done if I had found her there doesn't bear thinking about.' He added: 'I just hope she gets everything she deserves. She should be locked up and never allowed out. She's done much more than Myra Hindley.'

The church-loving parents of handicapped Timothy Hardwick took a gentler, Christian view. Before their son's death, Robert and Helen had both been in favour of hanging murderers, but the tragedy altered their opinion. 'We now think it's wrong to take a life for a life. You have to find it in your heart to forgive.'

Sue and David Peck had lost their only child, but were now preparing for the arrival of a new baby. The pregnancy had been a blessing, coming as it had as the police started their investigations. It had helped the couple cope with the aftermath of daughter Claire's death on Ward Four. Baby Jennifer Danielle was born safely at Kings Mill Hospital, Mansfield, on 29 February.

16. The 'Smoking' Syringe

While the parents were busy passing sentence, Supt Clifton and his team were still hard at it in the Incident Room.

He had amassed medical evidence that all pointed to Allitt; the DPP was confident the case was a strong one. But he hoped that, even now, he might yet find somebody who had seen Allitt with the 'smoking syringe'.

He turned his attentions to the events in the Jobson house where Allitt had gone to live for four months after he had first questioned her. He was particularly keen to know more about schoolboy Jonathan Jobson's mysterious collapse at the Sunday market.

There was new information, too, from the hospital where a full internal enquiry was under way. It was to reveal the name of yet another youngster who might have been a victim on Ward Four.

Seven-year-old Michael Davidson, who lived a mile or so from the hospital in Tamar Court, Grantham, had been just six when he was admitted to hospital with a .22 pellet wound in his stomach.

He had been shot accidentally as he played with his older brother's air rifle which neither of them realised was loaded. Luckily, the pellet missed all his vital organs and lodged underneath his liver. Michael underwent an operation and was recovering when he suffered a sudden and unexpected cardiac arrest.

Police had at first discounted him from the enquiry, believing he had hyperventilated as he was being given an injection of antibiotics by a woman doctor. The injection had seemed innocent enough because it had been given by a doctor and Allitt had not been in the room. But then the doctor told the enquiry she was no longer sure about her first diagnosis; she also revealed that the contents of the syringe had been prepared by Nurse Allitt.

Detectives re-checked Michael's case and were told by expert paediatrician, David Hull, that he was sure Michael had suffered a cardiac arrest. Michael's mother, Mrs Fay Davidson, said: 'I was told later the syringe had been passed to the doctor by a nurse.

'When I went to see him for the afternoon visiting he was fine. I left him sitting in the chair next to his bed at about 4pm. He was still on a drip but otherwise he was great. But by the time I had got home they were ringing from the hospital saying: "Get back up here." That was about 4.55. My other son and daughter-in-law were with him when he had the attack. So was the woman doctor.

'When the enquiry began at the hospital into the other children, she said she was not satisfied with what had happened to Michael. That's when they started an investigation into Michael's case. We didn't know about it until the police arrived at the house and told us they had found something that had caused him to collapse.'

Detectives believe the syringe contained potassium chloride, the poison they suspected had killed Claire Peck, though they could never be sure. But they were sure that Michael had been Victim No.13.

There was to be another, far more significant, development, an unexpected twist in the tail of the investigation.

All along, Supt Clifton had patiently probed the events on Ward Four, expecting that the attacks on the children would give him the conclusive evidence to convict Allitt.

But it was the mistreatment of a frail, old lady that was to prove crucial. The vital clue, the last important piece in the jigsaw, was discovered ten miles south-west of Grantham at an old people's home in the village of Waltham on the Wolds.

Allitt's former friend, Tracy Jobson, who had long since abandoned her after the events at her mother's home, told detectives how Allitt had spoken to her about her part-time job at the home. And she could remember how Allitt had told her that one old lady had been taken to hospital with hypoglycemia - a severe lack of body sugar. Could Allitt have turned her attentions from children to an old, helpless woman?

From the day the police arrived at the hospital there had not been another incident on Ward Four.

Now frail, seventy-nine-year-old pensioner Dorothy Lowe was to become the most important person in the long police investigation.

Allitt had only worked four shifts at the home, moonlighting to earn extra pin money. Five days after the death of fifteen-month-old Claire Peck, the last youngster to die on Ward Four, she had worked her third night-shift there. But, the next morning, Dorothy was so ill that a GP had been called at 7am and she had been rushed to the geriatric ward of Grantham and Kesteven Hospital with hypoglycemia.

Detectives began questioning other staff at the home, wondering what could have made the old lady so ill. And they discovered that Allitt had been seen giving her an injection of insulin.

Care assistant Alice Stewart told them she could remember seeing Allitt with a syringe in her hand giving an injection of insulin to Dorothy Lowe at about 5am. She had watched her put the syringe in her apron and walk away.

The old lady was a diabetic but had not been due to have her daily insulin jab until between 8am and 9am. It was a strict routine which was always carefully monitored.

Allitt had not recorded the injection on Dorothy's charts and there was no reason why it should have been given at least three hours too early.

Her insulin jab should have contained about eight or nine units. But experts at London's Guy's Hospital, who examined Dorothy's clinic notes, concluded that she must have been given about 100 units of insulin. The overdose could have killed her.

Supt Clifton was convinced he had finally found the 'smoking' syringe.

Detectives travelled to New Hall Women's Prison, Wakefield, on Wednesday, 11 March, more than ten months after the start of the investigation. There they read out six new charges to remand prisoner Allitt.

She was charged with attempting to murder Tracy's brother, Jonathan Jobson, aged fifteen, the boy who had loved her like a sister when she had stayed at his house.

She was accused of attempting to murder pellet-wound boy Michael Davidson, when he was aged just six.

And she was charged with attempting to murder Dorothy Lowe, aged seventy-nine, at the old folks' home.

Detectives accused her, too, of assaulting all three with intent to cause grievous bodily harm. This took the total number of charges she would face when she appeared before a jury to twenty-six.

On Thursday, 19 March, Allitt was committed, from the tiny Victorian Grantham Magistrates' Court, to stand trial before a jury at the Crown Court. The parents of the children of Ward Four had waited a long time for this moment. Peter and Sue Phillips, Chris and Joanne Taylor, David Peck, Hazel and

Robert Elstone, Stephen and Judith Gibson and Creswen O'Brien were among the fifty or so people who crowded into Number One court on the first floor of the Magistrates' Court.

Looking on from the back of the courtroom was Ruth Lindsey, the private detective whom Peter and Sue had recruited to help Allitt so many months before.

All the seats were full, snapped up long before Allitt was due to arrive from her cell at New Hall. Supt Clifton, who had stayed at his desk until 10.30pm the previous night to finalise the committal papers, had to stand on one side of the courtroom with colleague Neil Jones standing on the other.

Allitt was delayed en route to court for more than an hour. Finally, wearing blue jeans, a sweat-shirt and a track-suit top, she took her place in front of the bench at 11.10am. She sat between solicitor Mr Kendall and barrister Dudley Bennett; she showed no hint of emotion apart from nodding her head on being told she would stand trial at Nottingham, charged with all twenty-six offences.

Mr Bennett told the magistrates that the nurse, by now looking much leaner than when she'd first appeared in court in November, would be contesting all the charges. It was all over in the space of three minutes, and the families rushed outside to catch a glimpse of Allitt being driven away in a police van.

Sue Phillips managed to smile at the thought that justice was now in sight. 'We've waited so long, now at last she's got to face what she's done. I only wish the trial was tomorrow . . .'

Nurse Allitt was locked up in her Wakefield prison cell as Sue and Peter Phillips carried Katie into the pretty stone church at Manthorpe on Christmas Eve for her christening.

The Rev. Ian Shelton, who accepted the role of godfather, said a prayer for her sister Becky who lay buried a few yards away in the graveyard. Then he spoke of the miracle of little Katie's survival. She was now nearly eleven months old with a beautiful smile and an attractive tuft of blonde hair. Her survival had given Peter and Sue such joy and comfort after the nightmare of losing Becky.

Sue said: 'We have always been comforted by the thought that at least we have got Katie. Thank God she didn't take her too.'

But Sue and Peter had no idea that Katie, too, would also fall a victim to the curse of Nurse Allitt.

Sue began noticing a slight stiffness on Katie's right side, affecting her leg, hand and arm. She spotted her struggling to pass toys from hand to hand and, when she pushed herself along in her babywalker, she seemed to be using only her left foot. Her health visitor suggested physiotherapy, which would eventually get her muscles working properly. It was nothing to worry about, especially as she had been such a premature baby.

An appointment date arrived for Katie to be taken to Nottingham's Queen's Medical Centre for a routine check-up on 31 January – her first birthday. But Sue and Peter couldn't make the day and put the appointment back another month.

The specialist suggested that Katie be given a brain scan because he wanted to check whether any damage could have been caused by lack of oxygen on the night she'd 'died' for thirty-two minutes on Ward Four, even though she had seemingly made such a wonderful recovery.

Peter and Sue watched as their daughter was given medicine to send her off to sleep; then she was wheeled off to the neurosurgery unit for the scan. They were told it should take about six minutes but it lasted more than twice that long. The results were devastating.

Peter said: 'The doctor said he didn't know how to tell us what they had found because he knew we had already been through so much with Becky. But he said he didn't know how Katie was alive. Her brain was severely damaged. What she had left was barely the size of a walnut.

'She was virtually blind in one eye, and he told us she would never be able to walk or talk. She had little feeling on her right hand side. She wouldn't be able to go to the toilet herself.'

Sue said: 'We had to ask him to repeat it, because I couldn't understand all the medical terms he was using, but the second time sounded even worse. I just went to pieces. I couldn't take it. I just couldn't stand any more. It was just awful.'

She added: 'I told him there must be some mistake because she'd seemed so happy. She'd always smiled and laughed a lot. She would say

236

"dadda" and she would blow us kisses. She can scoot along in her babywalker. Surely, they must have got it wrong?

'But he said he was sorry, there was no mistake. Katie might seem to be all right on the outside, but the scan had shown what was happening on the inside. He told us that the brain stem was all right and a small piece above it which controlled her intelligence systems. But the rest of her brain was dead. The cells had decayed and the brain was filling with fluid. It would just be a matter of time before she died.'

Katie, he told them, could live until she was twenty. Or she could die tomorrow. If she survived, she would almost certainly be confined to a wheelchair and if she was able to make sounds, she would never be able to formulate sentences.

There were moments of silence as the Phillips collected their jumbled thoughts, their minds whirring in virtual panic.

Sue and Peter wondered if there was a possibility that Katie might have been born with brain damage, nothing to do with the events on Ward Four. But the doctor told them that both Katie and Becky had been scanned at birth because they were premature twins – and both girls had been found to be perfectly normal.

The damage had occurred when she was aged between six and eight weeks – the time she'd collapsed in the Grantham and Kesteven Hospital. It was caused by the lack of oxygen supplied to her brain.

Peter felt his anger boil inside him to a level he had never felt before. He said: 'If Bev Allitt had been anywhere near that hospital at that moment, I would have killed her. I have never felt such anger. I just wanted to get my hands on her. How could anyone do this to both our little girls? We thought she was our friend. We did all we could to help her, and now she was taking Katie too.'

Sue cuddled Katie in her arms as she later said: 'We will give her all the love and help we can for as long as we have got her. She's so lovely. She looks as beautiful as any normal baby.

'We will have to take her three times a week to a specialist unit where they can help her to cope, and there are special toys she can get. But what kind of life will she have now?'

Back in Grantham, other parents whose children had survived the chilling events on Ward Four noticed odd things about their children.

Twin Patrick Elstone still wasn't developing as fast as his brother Anthony who had not suffered the same ordeal. Something seemed to be wrong, although parents Hazel and Robert hoped he would soon 'catch up'. Patrick had difficulty using one of his hands, was slow crawling and hated being cuddled.

Almost all the parents had instructed solicitors to begin an action for damages against the hospital and the health authority. For most of those whose children were alive, it had seemed a token gesture at first, one of those 'just in case' precautions. What they really wanted was for their children to be normal and suffering no long-term effects.

But it could be months, perhaps years, before they would know the extent of any damage their children had suffered.

Back home, Peter received a letter telling him his shotgun licence was about to expire and he would need to apply for a renewal. He had been a full-time soldier, and also a member of the volunteer Territorial Army, and he'd always been keen on guns. He kept up his licence so that he could practise his skills on local clay-pigeon shoots.

He sent in his £11 fee, plus four passport-sized photographs, signed by the Rev. Ian Shelton. The renewal would normally have been a matter of routine but the local police were taking no chances. A few days later a policeman arrived to ask him questions about his application. He wanted to know just what Peter would like to do to the person responsible for what had happened to twins Becky and Katie.

'I told him I wouldn't be a good parent if I told him that I would do nothing. I said I would like to watch her die, like I had watched Becky die. I wouldn't be human if I didn't feel like that.'

Grantham police later suspended his licence – until after the trial of Beverley Allitt.

Peter said: 'They were right to do it. The truth is I could kill her for what she's done.'

17. The Trial

As she awaited her trial Beverley Allitt came within a whisker of saving Peter Phillips the trouble of pulling the trigger.

Allitt had long mastered the art of making herself ill in her continuing efforts to attract both attention and sympathy but, while she was in jail in Wakefield, she came perilously close to ending her life. She spent most of her time in the prison's medical wing or under guard in the local hospital with a string of ailments and, as the weeks ticked by, doctors became increasingly concerned about her dramatic loss of weight. She was not eating and by the time she next appeared in court, this time in Nottingham, she looked a different person. She had slimmed down from more than twelve stones to little more than nine. Parents who travelled to court to see her gasped as she appeared in the dock. Gone was the chubby, overweight young woman they remembered from Ward Four. Instead, Allitt was looking fitter, healthier and happier than they'd ever seen her.

But the truth behind her weight loss became known weeks later. She was still not eating, despite pleas from prison doctors, her parents and her lawyers, and there were signs that she was suffering from the slimmers' disease, anorexia nervosa. Her worried parents were sent shopping to buy their daughter new clothes because she had wasted away from a size 16 to a size 8.

Finally, she was so ill that she was carefully moved from her hospital bed to Rampton, the high-security psychiatric hospital in north Nottinghamshire.

By now Allitt was painfully thin. Her chubby features had vanished. Instead, she was drawn and gaunt-faced, her eyes deep set and shadowed by black circles. Her weight had plumeted from more than 13 stones to a pitiful 6st 13lbs. She was withering away, barely half the woman she had been on Ward Four.

Lawyer John Kendall was at pains to stress that the move did not mean she was mentally ill or that she would be unfit to stand her trial. She was only going to Rampton because doctors and nurses there had better facilities to treat her.

In Corby Glen Allitt's grandmother was desperately worried. She realised that the waiting was taking a terrible toll, but she could not understand why Beverley had all but given up eating. 'They've told me how ill she was and she's lost so much weight. The waiting for the trial is getting to her – it's getting to all of us.'

She need not have worried. The move to Rampton provided her granddaughter with more luxurious facilities than she could have dreamed of in any women's prison. This was a hospital, not a jail,

and she enjoyed her own room with ensuite bathroom facilities instead of her green cell at Wakefield. She began taking enough liquids – glucose
and vitamins – to stop the decline. She would still
take no solids but her weight loss stabilized. Allitt
settled back to await her trial now fixed for
Nottingham Crown Court.

Back at Grantham strenuous efforts were being
made by the health authority, doctors and nurses
to pick up the pieces after the devastating publicity which followed Allitt's arrest. Worried about its
shattered image and teetering public confidence
in the hospital, the Regional Health Authority
appointed a firm of professional public-relations
consultants called Westminster Strategy, based in
London. Important questions were being asked by
parents: Why didn't the hospital act sooner? Why
did it go on for so long? How was Allitt allowed to
nurse so many sick children when she was only
just out of training? But there would be no
answers. The public-relations people put up a
stone wall. They had been advised by lawyers rep-
resenting the hospital to say nothing until the trial
was over. And even then they might say nothing in
case they prejudiced any appeal.

David Crampton, who had tried to get answers
since son Paul's three mysterious hypoglycemic
attacks, was as frustrated as anyone. 'Until the
hospital sits down and tells us precisely what
happened to our children, people will speculate
with half the facts, and get half the truth,' he said.

The enquiry team set up to look into the running, staffing and future management of Grantham and Kesteven Hospital reported back after ten months – but even its findings were ordered to be kept secret until the trial was over.

Dr Richard Alderslade, regional medical officer for Trent Regional Health Authority, announced that his hands had been tied by the restraints of his lawyers. He said: 'Our intention was to publish a summary of the enquiry report and its full recommendations.

'We have been advised by our lawyers, however, that publication at this stage might interfere with the proper conduct of the trial of Beverley Gail Allitt and therefore could be contempt of court.'

He added: ' This is a matter of great regret. We cannot disregard the advice given.'

Parents were convinced that too much was being hidden from them. And the lack of openness made them even more frustrated. In the meantime, Martin Gibson, the hospital's administrator with ultimate responsibility for Ward Four, the man who had first called in the police a week after the death of final victim Claire Peck, was promoted to a new job in Leicester while the enquiry team was still carrying out its investigations.

Mr Gibson's successor, Allister Stewart, arrived as the future of paediatrics in Grantham hung in the balance. There were genuine fears among nurses and doctors that the awful events which had spanned those sixty dreadful days might lead to the enforced closure of the Children's Ward with services moved to another hospital. The ward was to survive – but only just.

In September 1992, almost a year after Nurse Allitt's arrest, staff from the Queen's Medical Centre in Nottingham were asked to take over the running of all children's health care in Grantham. The ward would remain open but it would be run by another hospital twenty-five miles away.

Union official Jenny Flood described the takeover as a 'slight on the people of Grantham'. She added: 'I believe it will do nothing to restore public confidence in the local service or indeed restore the shattered staff morale.' Hospital general manager, Mr Stewart, put on a brave face. He said: 'We are delighted that paediatric services will remain local and we recognize that the service will benefit from having a link with a centre of excellence.'

On Monday, 15 February, 1993, two years after the first death that of seven week old Liam Taylor on Ward Four, Beverley Gail Allitt walked into the dock in Court One at Nottingham Crown Court. There had been such a clamour for seats in the courtroom that a ticket system had been introduced and a loudspeaker relay was linked to an 'overflow court' set up temporarily in the pressroom.

The stage was set for a dramatic trial though the judge, Mr Justice Latham, could not know the dramas that would unfold in the weeks ahead as he took his place, resplendent in his red robes.

Before him was prosecutor John Goldring, QC, and defence counsel, James Hunt, both of whom had spent months preparing for this moment. Both counsel had junior barristers, for the prosecution Nigel Rumfitt and, for the defence, Dudley Bennett, ready to help analyse every shred of evidence in the weeks and months ahead. Allitt's solicitor, John Kendall, sat with a mountain of files at his feet on the back row of the legal benches, closest to the dock.

As it turned out, all those touched most by the case were missing. Allitt's parents, Richard and Lillian, had been advised to stay away; it was felt the trauma would be too much to bear. The parents of all the children who had suffered were also absent. They were to be called as crucial prosecution witnesses and were not allowed, therefore, to attend in case their evidence was affected by what they heard in open court. Instead they would sit at home, reluctantly forced to follow newspaper and television reports of the trial.

A hush descended as Mr Justice Latham announced: 'Bring in the defendant'.

If Beverley Allitt had been dreading this moment – as surely she must – there was no sign of it. At 12.05pm she walked through the door at the back of the dock into court with her head high, flanked by two women nurses from Rampton. She had been in custody for 453 days. Every eye in the courtroom focused on her gaunt, elfin face, her fair hair cropped boyishly short. She wore blue trousers with a white shirt and blue cardigan which hid her skeleton frame, ravaged by the effects of her anorexia. There was not a hint of colour in her ashen-white cheeks.

Allitt avoided every gaze, staring blankly, straight ahead of her in the direction of the judge. There was not even a flicker of emotion, no sign of nerves, as one by one the members of the jury – seven men and five women – took their places, each of them warned to expect a trial lasting up to three months. Here before them was a woman who, if they convicted her, would go down in legal history as Britain's worst woman serial killer, accused of more murders than even infamous Moors murderess Myra Hindley.

But was she guilty? The prosecution was in no doubt that she was. He spent a day and a half telling the jurors how the nurse standing before them had systematically attacked one innocent, sick child after another. No one had seen her do it. Nobody had witnessed her dreadful attacks. It wasn't even possible to be sure exactly what she had done to them. Some – Becky Phillips, Paul Crampton and the fragile old lady, Dorothy Lowe – had been deliberately injected with insulin. Others had collapsed when she had given them another drug or a cocktail of drugs; Claire Peck had been injected with a deadly dose of potassium chloride. With some she may simply have placed a hand over their tiny mouths to stop them breathing. Mr Goldring for the Crown, speaking calmly and without any emotive phrases, told the jurors: 'We cannot say in each case what the defendant did.

No one was watching her. Nurses are not expected to assault their patients.' Nor could he tell why she had attacked them. She had been trained at Grantham and Kesteven Hospital but had been off work so often, owing to various illnesses, that she had needed extra time to qualify as a nurse. She was also rejected by the nearby Pilgrim Hospital, Boston, and faced the grim prospect of being unemployed until Grantham had come to her rescue with a six-month contract on the Children's Ward.

On Ward Four there was a 'chilling pattern' to the attacks. Painstaking analysis of all the evidence revealed that Nurse Allitt was always there. She had been on duty on every occasion the children had collapsed. Youngsters had been safe when she was not at work. And the entire series of attacks had stopped upon her arrest.

There was damning evidence against Allitt. When the police began their enquiries they discovered that someone had tampered with the Ward Notebook, which was kept at the Nursing Station on Ward Four and used to make rough notes about patients. Mr Goldring said that someone had not wanted the police to see all the pages and had taken a pair of scissors to cut several of them from the book. It was no coincidence that the missing pages covered the period during which Paul Crampton, who had survived a massive overdose of insulin, had stayed on Ward Four.

Another medical record file, the Ward Allocation Book, which indicated which nurse had been assigned to which patient, had also disappeared from the ward. When the police searched Allitt's home, they had found it tucked in a bag in her wardrobe. Mr Goldring asked the jury: 'What was it doing there?', and commented 'Her explanation was wholly unconvincing.'

Detectives also discovered that the key to the ward's drug refrigerator, where various medicines (including insulin) were locked, had also strangely disappeared soon after Allitt arrived on the ward. She had been given a bunch of all the ward keys when she was on duty, but then reported that the fridge key was missing. All attempts to trace it had failed. Mr Goldring told the jury: 'You may come to the conclusion that she had taken the fridge key . . .also that she was less than frank about it all with the police.'

The diary of heart attacks, respiratory failures, deaths and lucky escapes, exposing the strengths and weaknesses of the prosecution case, was detailed by Mr Goldring. Liam Taylor, admitted with a chest infection, suffered a massive heart attack while he was being 'specialled' by Allitt. Mr Goldring alleged she had killed him either by administering a drug or a strong mixture of drugs or even by placing her hand over his nose and mouth to stop him breathing.

Timothy Hardwick, admitted after suffering an epileptic fit, was recovering while being nursed by Allitt, but within an hour he was dead from a heart attack. The prosecution alleged Allitt killed him, but they didn't know how.

Kayley Desmond, admitted with a chest infection and feeding difficulties, collapsed and stopped breathing three times while being nursed by Allitt. Air had been pumped into her right armpit. The prosecution alleged that Allitt had taken a syringe into her cubicle and deliberately injected her, Kayley survived.

Paul Crampton, admitted with a chest infection, collapsed three times with massive hypoglycemic attacks – a dramatic drop in his blood sugar-level – while Allitt nursed him. She had injected him with a huge overdose of insulin equal to a full adult syringe. Paul should have died but he survived.

Bradley Gibson, admitted with bronchopneumonia, was alone with Allitt when he suffered a massive heart attack and 'died' for thirty-two minutes. The prosecution said they believed he had been poisoned through his drip feed with an unknown drug or a mixture of drugs. Bradley survived.

Henry Chan, admitted with a fractured skull after falling from an upstairs window at home, was alone with Allitt when he stopped breathing and turned dark blue. The prosecution claimed Allitt had placed her hand over his nose and mouth as he slept. Henry survived.

Becky Phillips, was sent home from Ward Four after treatment for vomiting. She died the same night at home. The prosecution alleged that Allitt injected her with slow-acting insulin on Ward Four, either under the skin or into a muscle. She died from a massive hypoglycemic attack.

Katie Phillips, admitted purely for observation, was being 'specialled' by Allitt when she turned blue and stopped breathing. The prosecution alleged Allitt had suffocated her with a hand over her mouth and nose. Katie also had five broken ribs caused by Allitt squeezing her so hard it would have also stopped her breathing. Katie survived two more attacks. But she suffered severe brain damage.

Michael Davidson, admitted after being accidentally shot in the stomach with an airgun, collapsed after a doctor injected him with a syringe prepared by Allitt; this caused his heart to stop. The prosecution alleged that Allitt had tampered with the drug. Michael survived.

Christopher Peasgood, admitted with a chest infection, turned blue and stopped breathing seconds after being left with Allitt. He recovered, then collapsed a second time with Allitt at his side. The prosecution said it was 'not simply coincidence' that he had collapsed the moment Allitt took over. She must have interfered with his breathing. Christopher survived.

Christopher King, admitted with vomiting, was alone with Allitt when he turned blue and stopped breathing. The prosecution alleged that Allitt used asphyxiation or a drug. Christopher survived.

Patrick Elstone, admitted with diarrhoea, stopped breathing and turned blue; his emergency alarm had been switched off. Patrick survived but with serious and lasting damage.

Claire Peck, admitted with asthma, was alone

with Allitt when she stopped breathing and turned dark blue. She recovered. Then she collapsed again while Allitt was alone with her. The prosecution alleged that she was poisoned with potassium, either injected or introduced through her drip.

Dorothy Lowe, a resident in an old people's home where Allitt worked in her spare time, suffered a hypoglycemic attack. Allitt was seen giving her an unscheduled injection of insulin. She survived.

Jonathan Jobson, collapsed while on a trip to a Sunday market with Allitt and his mother Eileen. The prosecution alleged that he suffered a hypoglycemic attack after Allitt doctored a soft drink with insulin-producing tablets. Jonathan survived.

As the story unfolded, Allitt sat almost transfixed as if she had switched off. Very occasionally she flicked a darting glance in the direction of the jury. Mr Goldring, anticipating the inevitable question in the jury's mind, raised the issue of motive. He said: 'Why should a nurse do these things? The short answer is, we do not know. If you are satisfied she did it, you must convict her, even if you are baffled as to why'.

He went on: 'You must not speculate on her mental state in your verdict. You have to decide, did she do these things? Not why'.

Mr Goldring began calling the evidence. One after another the parents were called into the witness box, giving evidence just a few yards across the court from where Allitt was sitting. For some it was too much of an ordeal to bear. Sue Peck was so upset she couldn't face it, and her statement had to be read to the jury. Chris Taylor choked back his tears. Mercifully his wife Joanne was spared the ordeal when she was not called. But she broke down in the public gallery and had to be led from court. Nobody knew just how much her emotions were in turmoil. She had only just been told that she was expecting another baby.

Doctors, nurses and medical experts followed the parents into the witness box. The saddest must surely have been paediatrician Dr Nannayakkara. The jury heard how he had been so unhappy with the post mortem results on the very first victim, Liam Taylor, that he had pleaded for a specialist paediatric pathologist to check the findings, but his request had been turned down. He also told how much he regretted bringing perfectly well Katie Phillips into the hospital for checks after the death of twin sister Becky. He told the jury: 'I wish now I hadn't'.

The trial was entering its fifth week when it came to a sudden halt. Allitt collapsed at Rampton while the court was in recess for three days for legal argument. She was rushed to the Bassetlaw Hospital at nearby Worksop in Nottinghamshire where doctors battled to keep her alive. Her barrister, Mr Hunt, announced that she was suffering from the severe effects of anorexia nervosa. She was being fed through the nose by 'nasal gastric tube' and she was 'grossly underweight'.

Back in Grantham, the parents who feared the trial was about to be abandoned were furious. They were convinced it was just another cynical piece of theatre from Allitt's repertoire of feigned illnesses; a clever attempt to gain sympathy and escape justice. Chris Taylor was damning in his condemnation. 'She's just a very wicked and evil person. I'm sure she is just putting it on'. Sue Phillips snapped: 'She's just making herself ill again. It's what she's been doing for years'.

Back in court Mr Justice Latham and the two counsel were presented with a legal dilemma. How could the trial carry on without a defendant in the dock? After the months of detective work, painstaking analysis by the world's medical experts and the agonizing ordeal of the families, was it about to end with no verdict at all? Allitt herself provided the answer. When Mr Hunt visited her in the specialist psychiatric wing at Bassetlaw Hospital she declared that she was willing for the case to continue in her absence, even though she would not be in the dock to hear the evidence against her.

When the court resumed on 22 March there was an empty chair in the dock where Allitt should have been sitting. Later she wrote a long letter to the judge explaining that she was fit to give instructions to her lawyers but she did not want to give evidence herself to the court from the witness box. Instead, she would leave it to her Counsel to present her defence. She also made it clear that she would not have wanted to give evidence herself, even had she been well enough to do so.

Instead, it was left to police officers to tell the jury just how strongly she had protested her innocence when she was questioned by them. She told them she had done nothing wrong. In one interview with Detective Inspector Neil Jones she had told him: 'It can't be no fault I'm making. What can I do deliberately to do it? I wouldn't know what to do. Something has happened, yes, but I just can't help being there, can I?'

The Inspector told her: 'You are a young lady, just been made an enrolled nurse. Have you got to prove your credibility on that ward or show them you are the best one?'. Allitt replied: 'I have got nothing to prove. I just want to be a Staff Nurse. That is as far as I go'.

In five hours of taped questioning she still denied committing any offences. When she was asked about the attack on Paul Crampton she insisted: 'I told you. I didn't do it. I am telling the truth – God's honour. I deny giving him anything whatsoever, other than the medication prescribed. I would not give anything maliciously'.

The detectives asked her if she had a problem, to which Allitt replied: 'I tell you what. I will see a psychiatrist if you want, and I will talk to them. There is no problem.' She added: 'I am just fed up. I am being accused of something what I haven't done and I wouldn't dream of doing. I cannot get it through to nobody. No matter what you say, I am sticking to my story, I didn't bloody do it. I am not bloody lying. Everyone on that ward knows how much nursing means to me. It means more than living.'

* * *

During the trial, Sue Phillips kept her mind occupied by snipping newspaper cuttings and typing notes for her bulging files in which she recorded everything that had happened. Giving evidence in the witness box, though she was outwardly clear and strong, had tested the very depths of her drained emotions at the end of nearly two years of torment since Becky's death and Katie's miraculous escape. But somehow the mere task of recording every detail, her determination to miss nothing, helped numb the pain of the memories the trial had brought flooding back.

It was while she was busily typing in her dining room that Sue felt she was being watched. She wasn't sure what made her look round at the glass partition dividing the room from the hallway, except that she was convinced that someone was there. She decided that husband Peter was playing jokes and walked into the lounge, only to find him dozing on the settee with Katie sleeping quietly in his arms. It clearly wasn't him. Sue decided to carry on her work, but moved seats, so she was facing the glass partition.

What suddenly appeared before her made her gasp. In the glass just four feet in front of her appeared a face, staring at her from the hallway. Then it was gone. Sue ran into the lounge, expecting to find Peter laughing at the joke. But he was still asleep with Katie. She thought she heard a noise in the room above and dashed upstairs. But four year old son Jamie was asleep in his bed. Sue said: 'I felt such a fool. I was so convinced that the face was real but I knew it must be my imagination after all the tensions of the trial. I kept thinking: "Oh! God! I'm seeing things now". I knew I'd got to pull myself together or I would think I was going mad.'

Sue went to the kitchen and made herself a cup of tea. When Peter woke up, she made a joke of it and they both laughed. The next morning, little Jamie was getting ready for school when he announced: 'Becky came to see me last night, mummy. She came to my bedroom and talked to me'.

Sue recalls thinking she was going to faint. Becky had been dead for two years. They had buried her in a white coffin with her teddies alongside; Sue could remember tossing a red rose into her grave. Jamie was aged two at the time but he was always closer to Becky than he was to her twin sister Katie.

Sue said: 'When I found my voice, I asked Jamie what Becky was like. He said she often came to see him. He said: "She different now, Mum. She's got long blonde hair and she can walk, not like Katie." 'He told me when she went to see him at night, Becky had a glowing light behind her head. I've never believed in anything like this before and I felt a mixture of fear and excitement inside me. I just knew that Becky had come home.'

Sue and Peter decided to consult their vicar, the Rev. Ian Shelton, who had given them so much comfort previously. Becky was buried in his churchyard and he had conducted her funeral service. Sue told him she wasn't frightened and she didn't want anything done that would force Becky out of her home. She certainly didn't want an exorcism to drive out her spirit.

It was in February 1993 that Ian Shelton arrived at their home to carry out a service of Blessing with Sue and Peter. Sue said: 'We prayed that Becky would always be welcome, whenever she wanted to come home.'

Beverley Allitt spent the remainder of the trial in the relative comfort of her room at Rampton complete with television and en-suite bathroom. She was effectively 'off sick' as she had been for so much of her training as a nurse.

During her two years as a student at Grantham, Allitt had missed a total of 191 days through sickness, 94 of them in 1990, although this had not kept her away from hospitals. She admitted herself so many times to accident and emergency departments with cuts, sprains and illnesses that staff became convinced that she was deliberately inflicting the misery on herself. In all, she was treated twenty-nine times at hospitals in Grantham, Boston, Great Yarmouth and Peterborough.

She complained fictitiously she was pregnant or suffering from a brain tumour or ulcers. Several times she made repeat visits as her wounds strangely became re-infected or stitches ripped open. A hospital physio was so concerned about the volume of her visits that she warned the authorities in Grantham that she suspected Allitt was suffering from Munchausen syndrome but nothing was done. Owing to strict rules on the confidentiality of patient's records, none of the information about her hospital visits could ever be passed on and Allitt was allowed to carry on nursing.

The judge, Mr Justice Latham, would not allow evidence of Munchausen syndrome to be given to the jury fearing it would make it impossible for Allitt to have a fair trial. The jury finally retired to consider their verdicts at lunchtime on the forty-fifth day of the trial. The parents, now packed into the public gallery, drew comfort from one another. They were bound together in their suffering.

The verdicts took almost a week to deliver. Each one in turn brought tears and cheers from the waiting families: guilty to the murder of 'Little Pudding Pants' Liam Taylor, guilty to the murder of twin Becky Phillips, guilty to the murder of Claire Peck, guilty to the murder of 'My Special Boy' Timothy Hardwick.

The jury found her guilty too of attempting to murder Paul Crampton, Katie Phillips and Bradley Gibson. They also found her guilty of attacking Kayley Desmond, Henry Chan, Patrick Elstone, Christopher King, Michael Davidson and Christopher Peasgood, causing them grievous bodily harm with intent. But the jury cleared her of charges of attempting to murder and causing grievous bodily harm to Jonathan Jobson and Dorothy Lowe.

The judge ordered that Allitt should be brought from Rampton to the dock at Nottingham Crown

Court to be sentenced. The law dictated only one punishment – life imprisonment. The parents too faced their own life sentence, each family scarred forever by the dreadful memories of what happened in sixty days on Ward Four.